STAGE LIGHTING EXPLAINED

Neil Fraser

The Crowood Press

First published in 2002 by
The Crowood Press Ltd
Ramsbury, Marlborough
Wiltshire SN8 2HR

© Neil Fraser 2002

British Library Cataloguing-in-Publication Data
A catalogue record for this book is available from the British Library.

ISBN 1 86126 490 9

Dedication
This book is dedicated with much love to my mother and father – Jean and Keith. Also to my aunts and uncles who have always been a great pleasure to know and who, in particular, bring to mind many fond childhood memories – with love to Beryl, Jean, Ian, Betty, Peggy, and in memory of Bob and Ron.

Acknowledgements
Thank you to all those who have supplied or appeared in photographs. Theatre Companies: Contact Theatre in Manchester, Pavilion Theatre in Dublin, Polka Theatre in Wimbledon, Torch Theatre in Milford Haven, Soho Theatre and Westminster Theatre in London. Manufacturers: Lee Filters, Selecon Lighting, Strand Lighting, ETC Lighting, Vari*Lite UK. Individuals: Nicholas Barter and the staff and students at the Royal academy of Dramatic Art, Neil Irish, Bruno Poet, Jonathan Pearce and Nona Shepphard. Special thanks to Gary Thorne, Shirley Matthews and Kate Jones for help and inspiration. And extra special thanks and love, as ever, to Alex, Holly and Leanne.

Photographic Acknowledgements
Front cover: Tamsin Weston and Jason Cheater in *Dona Rosita, the Spinster* by F.G. Lorca – Rada. Lighting Design and Photo: Neil Fraser.
Back cover: Scene from a Rada production of *A Month in the Country* by Turgenev. Photo: Rada Archive.

All stage lighting in productions by the author except where noted; all photographs in the text are by the author except:
Leanne Archibold, pages 59, 87 (top). ETC Lighting, page 38. David Bishop, page 46. Holly Fraser, page 53 (top). Fokke de Hoog, page 54 (top). Lee Filters Ltd, page 70. Jonathan Samuels, page 50. Rada Archive, pages 4, 41, 103, 139, 140 (top), 141, 142 (middle & bottom). Selection Lighting, page 35. Strand Lighting, pages 36, 37. Vari*Lite Europe, page 31.

Line drawings by Keith Field.

Typefaces used: Cheltenham Bold Condensed (chapter headings), Photina MT (main text) and Helvetica (labels).

Typeset and designed by D & N Publishing, Baydon, Marlborough, Wiltshire.

Printed and bound in Great Britain by J.W. Arrowsmith, Bristol.

CONTENTS

FOREWORD

by Nicholas Barter

Neil Fraser's book on lighting and its design for the theatre is more than a technical handbook. It deals with the very essence of the live performance – for what we see is what we understand and Neil addresses the aesthetic of the visual in a fresh and stimulating way, tracing the history of how we look at the stage, at actors and at the sets that decorate and describe the play.

In an increasingly technical age, when sophisticated effects and the wonders of the digital memory boards have increased the capacity to charm an audience's eyes, it is all the more useful to be reminded of the basics of the craft when human ingenuity and a creative imagination can still make the simplest of performance space a place of power and the human spirit.

I can unhesitatingly recommend this book to directors as well as those with a specialized interest in lighting design.

Nicholas Barter in rehearsal.

INTRODUCTION

There is nothing ugly; I never saw an ugly thing in my life. For let the form of an
object be what it may – light, shade, and perspective will always make it beautiful

John Constable

This book is about the designing of light for theatrical performances. In my experience most professional lighting designers seem to agree that the best way to learn about designing lighting for the stage is by doing it. I believe this to be true.

However, we must not forget that part of the 'doing' involves preparation, method and applied knowledge. This book hopes to provide all these, but more than that it also deals with that other aspect of 'doing' – thinking.

Amongst the now considerable number of technical books on stage lighting, all seem to deal more with *how* lighting on stage works rather than *why*. The 'nuts and bolts' of stage lighting are well catered for, the ideas behind the equipment much less so. This book seeks to correct this.

This book includes a treatise of ideas for the seasoned theatre lighting designer and novice alike. It reviews the development of lighting in history, looks at modern practice and what has already been written about the subject, and seeks to define a theory of modern stage lighting design.

If nothing else it may be that, in railing at some of these ideas, vehemently opposing them perhaps, the reader can go on with their own work all the more resolved in their own opinions.

Thus this book serves as an overview of a complex subject that previously may have only partly been investigated by the reader.

For those who do dabble in the magical art of playing with light, this book may also serve as a number of things:

* a treatise on how to think about lighting rather than just feel about it;
* a guide to the ideas that have formed our modern practices;
* a rounding up of ideas explored but not consolidated;
* a broadening out of experience;
* a second opinion on discoveries and ideas already made.

Lighting design may or may not be an art form. In debating this issue we finally realize that the question is futile, and not one that really needs resolving.

Theatre lighting is a collaborative venture. It is what it is, part of the process that produces and enhances dramatic art. An occasionally frustrating, but ultimately highly rewarding adventure – now read on.

1 A LIGHTING HISTORY

INTRODUCTION

Even a glance at the development of early dramatic practice reveals practitioners who were preoccupied with, amongst other things, light on stage. Many ideas that we may have formed concerning the use and function of modern lighting on stage have often already been discussed or touched upon any number of times within this long history.

Frontispiece from Sabbattini's 1638 book on theatre design and machinery.

The very early history of technical theatre deals as much with the problem of how to get a decent amount of light on stage, as with what to do with it once it gets there. Nevertheless, the evidence shows that the discussion had begun.

Quotes in the early part of this chapter give a fascinating insight into this world. A world before electricity, where the means to control light or project it were crude or non-existent.

Surprisingly, even with such slender means at their disposal, early practitioners were often worrying about the same things, or coming to the same conclusions as ourselves (*see* Sabbattini on footlights, or Di Somi on the lighting of comedy and tragedy). Perhaps this is not so surprising. After all, little has fundamentally changed in the relationship between viewer and viewed. Since the earliest days, since theatre came off the streets and in from the outdoor arena – since the sixteenth century at least – the audience has remained physically removed from the action and in need of help to see and understand clearly the events before them. Perhaps the really astonishing thing is how little has really changed.

It must also be said that even in the days of candle, oil and, eventually, gaslight, the 'lighting technicians' of various periods still managed to create immensely wonderful and imaginative effects. They did not consider themselves lacking in equipment or scope to experiment. At various periods certain creative stage moments have probably never been bettered, Sadly, in many cases, the methods used to create them are often lost in the mists of time. But this is not always the case, as this chapter will hopefully demonstrate.

Interestingly on this theme the great English dramatic theorist Edward Gordon Craig (*see* page 16) in his book *Books and Theatres* takes a whole chapter to lament the wonderful texture and illumination of the bygone world of candlelight.[1]

We can do a lot worse than learn about the brilliant achievements of the theatre of the Italian Renaissance, the use of light for effect in the English Masque, the Spectacles of the Court of Louis XIV, or the creative, dramatic use of light in the American theatre of the nineteenth century. All these, and more, are worth studying for their moments of sheer genius in the realms of scenic illusion and the all-important creation of mood and atmosphere.

ANCIENT DAYS

Early dramatic performances occurred, for the most part, out of doors. Although the Greek encyclopedist of the second century AD Iulius Pollux mentions in his chapter on ancient Greek theatre that part of the theatre building was a 'lighthouse'[2] and whilst it has been conjectured that the dramatic self-blinding of Oedipus may have been carefully contrived to coincide with the final disappearance of the sun from the arenas of ancient Greece, we have no real evidence that such events occurred or that artificial illumination was used at all.

The birth of theatre in many diverse cultures and periods derived from religious ceremony, and one of the earliest references to theatrical lighting (of sorts) is in the writing of Bishop Abraham of Szuszdal who, in 1493, saw a presentation of the Annunciation in a Florentine church and marvelled at the hundreds of lights used to encircle the throne of God.[3]

Of the same period Giorgio Vasari (1511–74) described the manner in which such presentations were made – particularly those staged by the architect Filippo Brunelleschi (1377–1446):

> the apparatus of the Paradise of S. Felice in that city (Florence) was invented by Filippo (Brunelleschi) ... On high was a Heaven full of living and moving figures, and a quantity of lights which flashed in and out.[4]

In the same piece, Vasari goes on to describe the workings of these lights:

> above the heads of the angels were three circles or garlands of lights arranged with some tiny lanterns which could not turn over. These lights looked like stars from the ground, while the beams being covered with cotton resembled clouds.

Vasari goes on to describe another mechanism, which was:

> filled with small lights placed in many niches, and set upon an iron like cannon which, upon touching a spring, were all hidden in the hollow of the copper ... and when the spring was not pressed all the lights appeared through the holes there.

THE ITALIAN RENAISSANCE

Many ideas are first described in this period of high innovation and exploration. Indeed, in his writings, lighting maestro Richard Pilbrow (*see* page 95) describes it as 'the cradle of stage lighting'.[5]

Mobile candlelight, polished bowl reflectors, light coloured by silks and shone through liquid lenses (also colourable) are all catalogued in this period. Oil and flame are dimmed mechanically, and the use of footlighting in particular is recorded by Serlio (*see* below) as early as 1530.[6] In this period we know in

ABOVE AND OPPOSITE TOP: **Typical Renaissance perspectivized stage settings.**

particular of the work of three practitioners: Serlio, Sabbattini and Di Somi.

Sebastiano Serlio (1475–1554) published a book entitled *Regole generali di architettura*[7] in 1545 that deals with, amongst many things, a description of the artificial lighting of a typical Renaissance theatre to be erected within an interior – a courtyard or hall.

Serlio talks of 'general stage light', of 'mobile light' – the latter for specific effects like representation of the sun or moon. Torches and chandeliers are used and he mentions 'it is better to illuminate the scene from the middle ... A large number of lights are placed leaning at the front of the scene'.

Light is shone through glass bowls of liquid towards the stage and Serlio talks of colouring these liquids to create 'lights shining through, of divers colours'. Similarly water-filled bowls are used behind the light source as effective, but primitive, reflectors.

In using colour Serlio's thinking is not so far from modern ideas of colour use (*see* Chapter 6). Note the 'sad' equated with blue in this passage on making azure, which he says 'is like to a Zaphir, and yet somewhat fayre'.

> take a piece of Salamoniacke, and put it into a Barbers basen, or such a thing, and put water into it: then bruse and crush the Salamoniacke softly therein, till it be all molten, always putting more water unto it, as you desire to have it light or sad collour; which done, if you will have it fayre and cleare then straine it through a fine cloth into another vessell, and then it will be a cleare Celestiall blew, whereof you may make divers kinds of blew with water.

Interestingly, Serlio then goes on to describe the other two colours needed to make up the primaries green and red: 'emerauld collour' sees Saffron added to the mixture above 'as you would have it pale or high colloured'. 'Rubbie collour' is easy 'if you bee in a place where you may have red Wine' or else use 'brazill' that was a red wood 'beaten to powder'. For a lighter red 'red and white wine mingled together'. For lighter warm colours 'white wine will showe like a Topas or a Crisolite'.

Serlio then goes on to describe how to arrange the 'torches' in relation to the containers of coloured liquid for the best effects – particularly in terms of the amount of light being required.

Clearly these chandeliers will be used on or very close to the stage, projecting light from most vantage points: the wings, from inside the structures of the setting, and with also 'candlesticks above the Scene with great candles therein'.

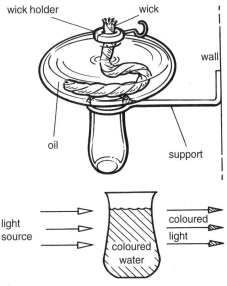

TOP: *The 'bozze', an early oil lamp.*
ABOVE: *Serlio's coloration of liquid.*

Serlio's long manuscript is a fund of interesting detail on the staging of his period. He describes many feats of staging and numerous scenic effects, amongst them the ability to produce smoke for effect and create the appearance of lightning.

Leone Ebreo Di Somi (1527–92) was in charge of court presentations in Mantua. Around 1556 he wrote a treatise on playwriting and theatre craft as a form of dialogue – questions and answers – between two courtiers.

In this document Di Somi makes fascinating points about the lighting of comedy and tragedy. He gets close to describing back-light, introduces the notion of mirror reflectors – although he comments that 'the ancients made use of them'[8] – and deals with the concept of contrast in lighting.

Dealing with lighting, Di Somi starts by describing the existence of 'so many hanging lights that one begins to see it (the scene) quite clearly, and it presents a very beautiful sight'.

One of his courtiers questions 'the purpose and origin of those many lights which are lighted on the roofs of the houses on the stage ... (elsewhere) I see torches in sufficient number to light the stage.' This could be taken as an enquiry doubting the use of light behind the performers (see back-light and its depth-enhancing properties, discussed on page 44). However Di Somi's reply is not absolutely clear: 'in the comedy ... the (stage) architecture also must represent happiness and joy. And ... as a sign of joy fires be lighted'. Literally – the more light, the merrier!

The question is then put: 'Will such lights be out of place, then, in tragedies?' After further comment on brightness representing happiness Di Somi replies:

'when the first sad event ... occurred ... I had ... the greater part of the lights on the stage which did not serve for the purpose of perspective, shaded or put out. This caused

very deep horror in the spectators' hearts. All of which ... achieved remarkable success.'

Next a question is put about the need for the light to be shaded from the audience: 'light that shines brightly in the eyes is extremely annoying' is the answer. But also that 'little mirrors, which are placed by some in suitable points in the perspective (set) prove both 'very attractive' and 'help, by their reflection, to make the scene appear more brilliant', as well as eliminating a source of eye irritation' by removing the light source and thus allowing 'lights without smoke'.

In contrast, Di Somi has the questioner ask why so many more lights are needed on stage than in the auditorium. The answer is given that 'it is natural that a man in the dark sees an object shining in the distance much better than if he were in a lighted place'. He quotes Aristotle as having made such a point. Going further he states: 'I place only a few lights in the hall, making the stage very bright. I place the few lights ... behind the listeners' backs, so that no interposed lights will interfere with their view'.

Nicola Sabbattini (1574–1654) built and equipped the Teatro del Sol in Pesaro that opened in 1636. Within the next three years, he published two books on the traditional practices of the theatre of his day. In these books Sabbattini wrote at some length on the subject of lighting, and interestingly made a strong case against the use, or overuse, of footlights.

In his first book, chapter 39 is entitled 'How to Arrange the Lights on Stage'. He comments on footlights thus: 'It is customary to arrange a great number of oil lamps in a row of footlights ... hidden from spectators by means of a board'.[9]

But he considers their use effects:

a loss greater than the gain. The intention is to make the stage brighter, but in reality it becomes darker – smoke develops (to such a

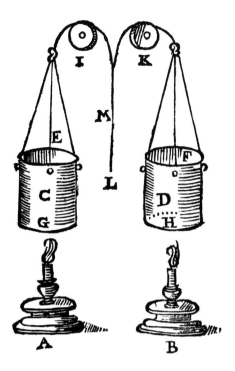

Sabbattini's dimming mechanism.

density that a sort of haze will interfere with the view of the spectators.

Which is to say nothing of the 'bad smell which emanates from oil lamps'. He goes on to deride the angle of light from the footlights:

> It is to be granted that the costumes of the actors and the dancers appear more striking, but it must also be admitted that their faces appear pale and lean ... besides the actors and dancers are blinded by the footlights.

In this period, lighting equipment is generally non-directional, and will be for some while to come. As such the auditorium is usually as well lit as the stage. Chapter 41 of Sabbattini's technical book is called 'How to Light the Lamps', and here he makes an interesting

---

Light Relief

On a lighter note, the writings of Sabbattini, in his dissertation on stage lighting of 1638, also noted that the falling down of scenery or of lamps (oil in this case) due to the clomping around on stage of performers or dancers 'is one of the things that damage the prestige of a stage director' – so, once again, no change there then!

---

distinction between the two. He says that when the performance is to start:

> lamps must be lighted, first those in the auditorium, then those on stage. Care should be taken that this is done as quickly as possible lest the spectators become uneasy and get the impression that the job will never be finished.

So no 10-second house light cues here!

Also worthy of study in this period are the writings of Angelo Ingegneri (1550–1631) and Josef Fürtenbach (1591–1667) The latter, a German who studied in Italy, wrote his *Architectura Recreations* in 1640. In it, his detailed description of the lighting of the period confirms the general layout that is to stay more or less unchanged until electric light sources finally make possible directional projected light. This layout has candlelight sources that are placed as close to the stage picture as possible; above, to the side and down on the front of the stage.

THEATRE LIT BY CANDLE

For a period from the earliest times until the nineteenth century, written descriptions of theatrical light in use deal mostly with the often vexing problems that Sabbattini mentions above – the care and use of candles. However, ideas are often expressed that resonate down the years to us today. In England throughout the period of the first performances of Shakespeare, the Globe and its sister theatres were not artificially lit, and thus performances took place in the daytime only. The courtyard performances of liturgical or other works were, however, a different case.

Inigo Jones (1573–1652), an English architect in the Italian mode, created spectacular settings for court masques. The libretto for 'Hymenaei', a masque in honour of the Earl of Essex, contains the comment that:

> the lights were so placed, as no one was seene; but seemed, as if onely Reason, with the splendor of her crowne, illumin'd the whole Grot.[10]

In the court of Louis XIV in France we find the same problem involving the speed of lighting changes and extinguishing candles.

Samuel Chappuzeau writes in his *Le theatre français*:[11]

> It is also the decorator's task to provide two candle snuffers if they do not wish to perform that job themselves ... they must perform the task promptly so as not to keep the audience waiting.

He also notes that they always to 'be keeping a watchful eye that the flats do not catch fire'.

In Venice, in 1683, a reporter writing in the *Mercure Galant*[12] describes a kind of 'dimmable' house lighting in use in the San Giovanni Cristostomo Opera House:

> An hour before opening ... whence descends a kind of chandelier ... (it) carries four great tapers of white wax, which light the auditorium and remain lighted until the curtain is raised. Then the whole machine vanishes ... As soon as the opera is ended, this machine appears again to light the auditorium.

THE EIGHTEENTH CENTURY

Francesco Algarotti (1712–64) wrote in his *Saggio l'opera in Musica*[13] about the practices of the French theatre world of 1755. He called for a number of reforms that he felt were needed to create a greater sense of illusion or stage moment. This included the concept of using chiaroscuro lighting (*see* Chapter 2, page 25). On this he says: 'What wondrous things might not be produced by the light, when not dispensed in that equal manner ... as is the custom'. He continues that by:

> distributing it (light) in a strong mass on some parts of the stage, and by depriving others ... at the same time; it is hardly creditable what effects might be produced thereby; ... a chiaro obscuro, for strength and vivacity, not inferior to that so much admired in the prints of Rembrandt.

Nagler comments that many of Algarotti's ideas were eventually taken up by the choreographer Jean Georges Novérre (1727–1810) at the Grand Opéra in Paris.[14]

In England, David Garrick (1717–79), the actor manager, is credited with bringing a number of innovations to the English stage from France, which he visited in 1764. For example, at Drury Lane Theatre, the following year (1765), he removed the unconcealed lights above the stage that had shone into the eyes of the audience.

THE NINETEENTH CENTURY – GAS AND ELECTRIC LIGHT

The following description expounds on the history and inventiveness of nineteenth-century theatre practice in a period that sees a veritable explosion in what is technically possible. I would also like to draw the reader's

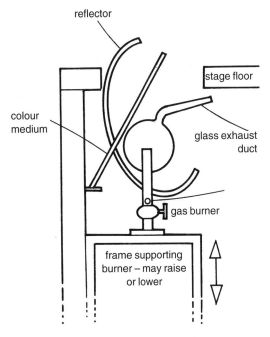

Typical gas footlight.

attention to the excellent book *Theatre Lighting in the Age of Gas* by Terence Rees for even greater detail and analysis – *see* Further Reading page 155.

Glynne Wickham in his historical writings evaluates the developments of this century thus:

> Candles and oil-lamps (had) provided the sole form of lighting in every theatre until the end of the eighteenth century, (they) were banished first in favour of gas and limelight and then in favour of electricity.

He adds that 'It was only with (the) invention of illumination by coal-gas that it became possible for a stage manager to control both the quantity and the direction of light.'[15] What follows chronicles the developments that occurred in this busy century.

1803 – the Lyceum Theatre in London becomes the first to use gaslight as part of its lighting.

1817 – Drury Lane Theatre is first to be totally lit using gas.

1826 – Limelight is invented, an oxygen and hydrogen mix burning on a block of lime. It becomes the first really bright light source, and is deemed sufficient to incorporate into, what we can now see as, an early directional spotlight. By the end of his career Walter Kerr (1809–93) has so dominated the use of this medium that he is dubbed the 'father of limelight'.

1843 – All London Theatres have converted to gas by this time, the Haymarket being the last.

1846 – Electricity is used to create a light source for the first time in the Paris Opera to spotlight a performer, but it is noisy and it flickers – limelight is preferred.

1855 – A lens is put in front of limelight for the first time.[16] This unit is generally used to follow performers, and thus, even today, follow-spots are still often referred to as 'limes'. Arc-light is also used in a similar way around this period.[17]

1863 – Charles Albert Fechter suggests concealing footlights, and Henry Irving adopts this practice for the first time at the Lyceum Theatre, London.

1878 – Incandescent electric light is used, for the first time in a theatre, in the Paris Hippodrome. It is silent and does not flicker.

1879 – The California Theatre in San Francisco becomes the first American theatre to be lit by electric light, using 1,158 lamps.

1881 – The Savoy Theatre in London becomes the first English Theatre to be lit with electric light.

1886 – The Paris Opéra is the first European theatre to be fully converted to electricity.

1889 – Henry Irving (1838–1905) introduces the notion of completely darkening the auditorium during performances, stating that 'stage lighting and groupings are of more consequence than the scenery.'[18]

Bram Stoker (of *Dracula* fame), who was Irving's assistant, writes 'It became an easy matter to throw any special part of the stage into greater prominence'.[19]

1896 – Kliegl Brothers were founded in New York. This was the first company specializing in lighting equipment.

1914 – Strand Electric was founded in England. It remains a leader in its field (*see* F. Bentham, page 93).

In the late nineteenth and early twentieth centuries there came a time when equipment devised to illuminate the stage reached a new level of flexibility and brilliance, and as such, the way lighting had been previously arranged and the thinking on it had to change.

As a result, a few people eventually saw a need to state their vision or basic understanding of how light could be used on stage. It is this moment that sees the first real complete 'theories' of stage lighting, theories that are still often of use to us today (*see* Chapter 8).

This moment in history also more or less coincided with, and could even be said to have derived in part from, a strong move away from the overbearing artifice of the nineteenth century – that is, a desire to break away from the 2D picture (set against a now darkened auditorium) that theatre had generally become. The new electric light made more than a small contribution to this aspiration.

Peter Brook wrote:

'The great days of painted scenery belonged to the era of dim lighting from gas-fed footlights or candles, which flattened the performer so that he and the picture became one. The day the first spotlight was hung on the side of the proscenium, everything changed: the actor now stood out, was substantial, and a contradiction suddenly appeared between his roundness and the two-dimensional trompe l'oeil behind his back'.[20]

THE TWENTIETH CENTURY AND BEYOND

In today's theatre world, we have an almost boundless freedom in the way in which we present and reinterpret drama on stage. Sometimes it is good to remember not only where this freedom has come from, but also just how wide it is.

In the technical arena our sense of freedom can, perhaps, be said to date from the ideas of two great men: Adolphe Appia and Edward Gordon Craig. Naturally, of course, their work did not arise in a vacuum.

Theatre practitioners of every century have sought to reinvent ways of making stage productions powerful and meaningful for their audiences – remember the 'deep horror in the spectators' hearts' caused by Di Somi in 1556 (*see* page 10).

As the twentieth century dawned, there came a reaction across Europe and beyond to what was perceived as the artifice of the nineteenth century. From Stanislavsky in Russia, George Fuchs in Germany, Jarry, Antoine and Zola in France, W. B. Yeats in Ireland, and Strindberg in Sweden, all wanted to do away with painted cloths and fake vistas, demanding, instead, 'real' things on stage.

Agreement and reaction to these theatrical philosophizers, and others in the allied arts, then led to the more abstract developments of Dadaism, Surrealism and, in the theatre, Symbolism. This, in turn, led others to turn to Expressionism and a breadth of other theatrical styles.

Thus the thoughts of Artaud, Tzara, Maeterlinck, the Bauhaus, Grotowski and Bertolt Brecht, in their different ways, paved the way for Beckett, Sartre, Ionesco, Pirandello, Pinter and Peter Brook, and the rich diversity of theatrical styles we know today.

Alongside this, inevitably, a new language had to be written for the devices of scenery, furniture, costume and, of course, lighting.

Not all the great theatrical revolutionaries of twentieth-century theatre actually dealt with lighting specifically – that is, perhaps, why Appia and Craig are so influential as, among the throng, Appia and Craig were, arguably, the clearest, the earliest and the most outspoken, in particular about how a new language of scenic art was to be achieved

Those that did comment on theatre lighting are easy to understand, especially from the context of our own time and work. What follows, in roughly chronological order, is a summary of the thoughts of the most influential of these people.

August Strindberg (1849–1912)

At the turn of the century the movement away from the counterfeit of scenic illusion was initially toward the 'naturalistic'. One of the best known declarations of Naturalism was made by playwright August Strindberg in the preface to his play *Miss Julie*[21] in 1888. In it he calls for realistic interior settings and for 'the abolition of the footlights'.

He says of footlighting:

> Does not this light from below tend to wipe out the subtler lineaments in the lower part of the face ... does it not give a false appearance to the nose and cast shadows upward?

He goes on to comment that it hurts the eyes of the actors and makes them pull unnatural faces. He asks further 'Would it not be possible by means of strong sidelights (obtained by the use of reflectors, for instance) to add to the resources already possessed by the actor', thus enhancing the actor's ability to use 'the play of the eyes'.

Adolphe Appia (1862–1928)

Appia, a Swiss stage artist and scenographer, wrote copiously about the need to re-evaluate the art of scenography. He anticipated the symbolic movement by deciding that the search for 'realism' was as artificial as what had preceded it.

Appia's major works appeared in print in 1895 and 1899,[22, 23] although his notable essay *Notes de mise en scene pour L'Anneau de Nibelung*, about the staging appropriate to the work of Wagner in Beyreuth, written in 1891, was not published until 1954.[24]

Appia called for scenery to be three-dimensional rather than simple painted cloths. Appia wrote that 'Painting and lighting are two elements which exclude each other'.[23]

Naturally, he envisaged lighting as playing a vital part in revealing the edifices. H. D. Sellman writing in 1930 says Appia also 'called footlights the monstrosity of our modern theatre.[25]

Appia wrote:

> What music is to the partitur, light is to the presentation ... an element of pure expression as contrasted with those elements that bear a rational meaning.[23]

Appia divided light into two groups:
1. Verteiltes Licht or Helligkeit (General Illumination.
2. Gestaltendes Licht (Formative Light).[23]

The first of these was the more traditional light, to be used to soften shadows and diminish contrast caused by the second. The second however – a new light for the theatre – was for creating 'relief, plastic form, for the actor and his environment, a concentrated beam of light cast from an ideal, predetermined position'.[26]

Peter Goffin, in his book *Stage Lighting for Amateurs* of 1938,[27] says Appia saw that 'light was the living theatrical element' and that it could provide 'a unity between actor and his environment'. But that this unity would only come about when 'solid stage forms, designed to provide special surfaces or planes for lighting would take the place of flat perspective painting'.

Appia experimented and discovered the importance of shadow to offset light – he:

planned his lighting with special regard to the use of shadow-masses, which not only emphasized the plasticity of the setting itself, but possessed an appropriate dramatic significance.[27]

George Fuchs (1868–1932)

Fuchs was a director of the Munich Art Theatre and his writings start from a very similar premise to those of Appia – that is, to do away with artificial attempts at the 'real'. However, unlike Appia, he thought that the performer should not be put in an abstract three-dimensional setting, but made three-dimensional by lighting against a two-dimensional backdrop. In his mind scenic painting still had a role.

The actor however should be defined by light; 'the most important factor in the development of stage design'.[28]

Edward Gordon Craig (1872–1966)

In England, Craig, like Appia, developed a philosophy of symbolic scenography ahead of its time. In fact both theorists were given little chance to actually try out their ideas. Indeed when Craig, who was more a thinker than a doer, came to try out some of his scenic ideas they were often technical disasters.

Craig, a producer/scenographer, published *On the Art of the Theatre* in 1911. In it he described a scene without the 'distraction of scenery' needing 'to create a place which harmonizes with the thoughts of the poet.[29]

Craig rather sidestepped the issue of lighting, saying 'I thought to tell you here something about the uses of artificial light; but apply what I have said of scene and costume to this other branch as well'.[30]

Once again a practitioner attacked what must be seen as the most artificial and overused element in the theatre they despise – the footlight. Craig wrote 'in place of the footlights another method of lighting faces and figures could be adopted'.[31] Provocatively Craig writes that it would be 'a blessing if the theatres were not only without footlights but without lights altogether'.[32]

Goffin comments that for Craig 'clearly, lighting and décor must provide no more than a simple, neutral background, leaving the imagination free to build as the ear hears'.[33]

Or as the English critic Arthur Symons (1865–1945) wrote, in his book of 1909, staging from the likes of Craig gives 'suggestion instead of reality, a symbol instead of an imagination'.[34]

Stanislavsky, Meyerhold and Komissarzhevsky

Constantin Stanislavsky (1863–1938), co-founded the Moscow Arts Theatre in 1897–98 and in him 'Naturalism' had one of its strongest advocates. Stanislavsky worked alongside Anton Chekhov and, another theorist, Vsevolod Meyerhold (1874–1940). In 1903, Meyerhold broke away from the strictures of Stanislavsky's belief in psychological truthfulness to establish a theatre which 'seized with unquenchable thirst would go in search of new forms for the expression of eternal mysteries.'[35]

Meyerhold developed ideas for his staging from the writings of Fuchs. In 1905, he returned to the Moscow Arts Theatre at the invitation of Stanislavsky to run the newly opened Studio, but with disagreements between them both, and the turbulent political environment of Moscow in that year, the Studio never opened.

Instead Meyerhold left to run a theatre established by the popular actress Vera Komissarzhevskaya. She is quoted as saying that theatre should show 'suggestions of things and not the things themselves'.[36] Her ideas were codified in a theoretical statement entitled 'The Dramatic Theatre of V. F. Komissarzhevskaya' written in fact by the poet and dramatist

Aleksandr Blok (1880–1921), who worked alongside Meyerhold.

Meyerhold was followed as director in his sister's theatre by Fyodor Komissarzhevsky (1882–1954). Seeking perhaps a compromise between Meyerhold's ideas and what was conventional at the time, Komissarzhevsky calls his approach 'synthetic' and, like others before him, strove for a scenically unified stage. He wrote:

> The rhythm of the music must be in harmony with the rhythm of the movements of the actors, of the colour and lines of the decors and the costumes, and of the changing lights.[37]

Futurism: Marinetti, Prampolini, Depero
Ironically, Futurism was too anarchic to have much of a great future! Its exponents failed to achieve or even seek great or lasting work in their fields. Instigated in Paris in 1909 by the writings of Italian Filippo Marinetti (1876–1944) his *Manifeste des auteurs dramatiques futuristes* states that theatre 'among literary forms, the one that can serve Futurism most effectively – (should) force the soul of the audience away from base everyday reality'. That it should be a world of 'terrestrial, marine, and aerial velocities, dominated by steam and electricity'.[38]

Marinetti's work was published in England in Edward Gordon Craig's magazine *Mask*. He met Meyerhold in Paris in 1913 and visited Moscow the following year to work in his studio. Meyerhold, Stanislavsky and their contemporaries were at some odds with Marinetti's rather extreme views.

In Italy, fellow theorists were more in accord, among them Enrico Prampolini (1894–1956) and Fortunato Depero (1892–1960)

Prampolini writes to denounce Appia and Craig as having only 'made some limited innovations, some objective syntheses'. He calls for a stage of

electro-mechanical architecture, given powerful life by chromatic emanations from a luminous source provided by electric reflections of multicoloured panes of glass, arranged and coordinated analogically with the psyche of each scenic action'.[39]

Similar extreme statements were made by Depero in his *Il teatro plastico* of 1910.[40]

Dada and Formism: Tzara and Witkiewicz
One of Futurism's offshoots or interconnected philosophies was the even more destructive Dadaist movement. Founded in Zurich, New York and eventually centred in Paris, one of its followers was Tristan Tzara (1896–1963). In 1922 he wrote:

> Actors could be freed from the 'cage' of the proscenium theatre, and scenic and lighting effects be arranged in full view of the spectators, making them a part of the theatre world.[41]

Stanislaw Witkiewicz (1885–1939) returned from visiting Paris (via the Russian Revolution) to his native Poland and became involved with the Formist movement in 1918.

A playwright, Witkiewicz wrote in *On a New Type of Play* of a synthetic theatre in which

> each element – a gesture, a colour, a musical note, a shaft of light – must be seen as a formal element and accepted not for itself but as part of this whole.

As with others before and after him, he saw an analogy between theatre and music. Seeing the elements that make up the performance being like 'a sequence of chords in a musical work'.[42]

Expressionism: Reinhardt, The Bauhaus, Gropius, Schreyer
Expressionism, although predominantly in origin a German movement, is a term defining a

broader approach than Dadaism or Futurism. It had neither a specific centre nor single body of followers.

The later work of Ibsen and Strindberg leaves 'Naturalism' behind in favour of an abstracted reality. Strindberg, in particular, became a major icon for Expressionism. *See* his *A Dream Play* of 1902.

Precursors of Expressionism included Georg Büchner (1813–37) and Reinhard Sorge (1892–1916), both of whom died before their time at the tender age of twenty-four. These playwrights found one of their greatest interpreters in director Max Reinhardt (1873 – 1943) whom J.L. Styan describes as 'possibly the greatest director of modern times'.[43]

The premiere of Sorge's play *The Beggar* was produced by Reinhardt in 1917. Of it a contemporary critic wrote:

> The staging showed an understanding of the expressionist mind; across the proscenium hung a fine gauze, that now familiar device for preventing the diffusion of light on a subdivided scene ... The lighting moved from one part of the scene to another, leaving all the unlighted part invisible.[44]

Reinhardt developed a series of 'spectacle' plays; one such, *The Miracle* was based in part on a work of symbolist Maurice Maeterlinck (1862–1949). Of this production one witness commented:

> streams of coloured light, yellow, blue, and white, flaming through the latticed surface of square black boxes or prisms posed on storklike legs. Forty-seven electric fans drove up the yellow silken ribbons upon which the light from the forty arc lamps beat. The shrieks of the revellers filled up the intervals of the fiery effects as they made themselves felt in the conflagration overhead. For some moments we stood in the midst of blinding lights, flashing flames, and crashing winds. The bell rang and there was the silence and darkness of death.[45]

Leading playwrights of the Expressionist movement include Ernst Toller (1893–1938), Frank Wedekind (1864–1918) and Georg Kaiser (1878–1945).

The main centre of exploration of Expressionism, especially in production techniques[46] was the Bauhaus, a school of design in Weimar. In 1921 Walter Gropius (1833–1969) was charged with running the institute and invited fellow theorist Lothar Schreyer (1886–1966) to develop a studio theatre there. Between them they wrote of this new venture and the expressionistic methodology they applied.

Gropius states in *Der Arbeit der Bauhausbühne* that a

> new scenic space should be based on the spirit of construction (*Bau-Geist*) and should unite movement, organic and mechanical bodies, form, light, colour, verbal and musical sound.

That 'an immaterial idea' (should derive from) 'movement and repose, optics and acoustics'.[47]

Schreyer asserts, more abstrusely perhaps, that theatre should be a 'mechanical means freed from mechanism, organic means freed from the organic, light and soul, the living parts of the work'.[48]

This movement eventually led directly to the work in Berlin of Erwin Piscator (1893–1966) and, one of the twentieth century's greatest theatre innovators and practitioners, Bertolt Brecht.

The USA – Belasco, Cheney, MacGowan, O'Neill

Working within Broadway's perhaps limited understanding of 'Naturalism', and far from the European extremes of Futurism and its offshoots, David Belasco (1859–1931) nevertheless stretched the limits of technical expertise in his stagings as perhaps never before – blizzards, hurricanes, radiating sunshine, dust storms and much more were painstakingly recreated on stage – or apparently so – and presented to an admiring public.

Belasco was also more than a little in accord with Appia and others in the prominence he conferred on stage lighting. In 1919, in his book *Theatre Through Its Stage Door*[49] he wrote that lighting

> is the all-important factor in dramatic production ... sunlit scenes imply happiness, moonlit scenes give a suggestion of romance, while tragedy or sorrow should be played in gloom..
>
> Lights are to drama what music is to lyrics of a song. No other factor that enters into the production of a play is so effective in conveying its mood and feeling.
>
> The greatest part of my success in the theatre I attribute to my feeling for colors, translated into effects of light.

Working often with lighting technicians (they were not yet called designers) Louis Hartman and David Warfield in New York, Belasco describes 'years of experiment' to secure the lighting effects he was striving for. Often using 'special reflectors ..., cloths... evolving colors by transmitting white light through gelatin or silk of various hues'. Of his production *The Darling of the Gods*, he describes using the effect of 'a great blood-red setting sun to symbolize ebbing life'.

Many more radical practitioners in the US found their voice in the magazine *Theatre Arts* founded by Sheldon Cheney in 1916. Sheldon championed the European experimentation and articles by Craig and Appia appeared.

Leading the American theorists at this time was playwright Eugene O'Neill (1888–1953) and Kenneth MacGowan (1888–1963). The latter wrote against realism and in support of a synthetic theatre – of 'a complex and rhythmic fusion of setting, lights, actors, and play.[50]

Into the 1930s: Pirandello, Barker, Baty, Artaud

Those playwrights who disputed the boundaries of theatrical expression in the 1930s included Luigi Pirandello (1867–1936) in Italy, T.S. Eliot (1888–1965) and Harley Granville-Barker (1877–1946) in England, and in France Gaston Baty (1882–1951). The latter wrote:

> If the theatre wishes to present 'an integral vision to the world', it must use plastic expression, colour, light, music, gesture, and so on, to evoke the world beyond the word and text.[51]

A later influential figure in this period was Antonin Artaud (1896–1948) who saw theatre as a tool for revolution, as the ultimate means to change human existence, and who described a 'Theatre of cruelty' in his various manifestos of the 1930s.

Also, writing at the end of his career, Stanislavsky continued to be influential. And then came Brecht!

Bertolt Brecht (1898–1956)

Brecht is one of the undoubted giants of twentieth-century theatre. He was exiled from Nazi Germany in 1933 but invited back to East Germany to found the Berliner Ensemble in 1949. He continued to work with them until his death.

Brecht wrote prolifically about his work and ides, setting out several 'models'. He took the ideas inherent in the expressionistic work he saw around him in Germany in the 1930s and went on to develop a theatre of his own – best described as 'Epic Theatre'. This was a theatre of politics and reportage. Brecht shunned any of the glamorous or romantic ideals inherent in the work that preceded him.

He dealt with a theatre of ideas rather than emotions. 'What good' he said 'was the finest lighting equipment if it lit nothing but childish and twisted representations of the world?'[52]

To this end Brecht's most famous concept was that of *verfremdungseffekte* – usually translated as 'alienation effect'. This involved using a repertoire of theatrical methods and tricks to remind the audience, or keep them aware, that they were in an artificial environment. That they were required to think about what they were watching and not get too emotionally involved

In lighting, and indeed in scenic terms, Brecht did two things. Firstly, he kept things unromantic and uncomplicated – bare stages, simple curtains and bright unsophisticated lighting. In a production of *Antigone* he calls for acting areas 'simply to be brilliantly lit'.[53] About *Mother Courage* in 1949, he said,

Our lighting was white and as brilliant as our equipment allowed. This enabled us to get rid of any atmosphere such as would have given the incidents a slightly romantic flavour.[54]

Actor Robert Demeger playing the eponymous hero in Contact Theatre's production of **Brecht** *with Eve Matheson.*

Methuen's 1970s collected Pinter. Note the surrealist covers.

Styan states Brecht required that 'The stage itself would be lit with a plain white light so that the actor would seem to be in the same world as the audience'.[55]

Secondly, Brecht used whatever means he could think of to keep the audience 'alienated' – signs, coarse scenic devices, 'coloured projections were thrown on the cyclorama',[54] asides to the audiences, political songs unrelated to the storyline, and sharp abrupt changes of lighting. This also included allowing the equipment itself to be in full view of the audience. He wrote 'There is a point in showing the lighting apparatus openly, as it is one of the means of preventing an unwanted element of illusion.' He said that by so doing 'we destroy part of his (the viewer's) illusion of being present at a spontaneous, transitory, authentic, unrehearsed event'. Once again Brecht also asked for 'brilliant light' to complete the effect.[56]

The Absurd – Ionesco, Adamov, Beckett, Sartre, Pinter

It was Martin Esslin who famously grouped several writers and thinkers together under the title *Theatre of the Absurd*.[57] Although all worked independently of each other, and in variously different styles, nevertheless these playwrights had in common the manner in which they continued to explore the dramatic freedoms possible in the theatre of the twentieth century.

They built on Strindberg's theatre of dreams, on Brecht's refusal to use the traditional 'romantic' story-telling methods, providing works that at last suited the flexible, symbolic, and non-real settings of Appia and Craig. The key text was perhaps Beckett's *Waiting for Godot*, premiered in French as *En attendant Godot* in Paris in 1952.

Jerzy Grotowski (b. 1933)

In Poland, director Jerzy Grotowski took Artaud's theories of 'cruelty' into new areas. He wrote that:

the essence of theatre lies in the relationship between the 'poor theatre', opposed to the synthetic rich theatre that betrays this essence by attempting, in vain, to unite literature, painting, sculpture, architecture, lighting, and acting in a 'total theatre' experience.[58]

For technical innovation I would also direct the reader to the work of Mariano Fortuny (1871–1948) in Spain, with his work on colours transmitted through silks, and Josef Svoboda (b. 1920) the Czech scenographer who used projection, and powerful (low voltage) back and toplight units to create a style of lighting that was integrated with the scene it lit.

Peter Brook (b. 1925)

In the UK, Peter Brook explored a rich abstract setting in, amongst others, his famous production of *A Midsummer Night's Dream* for the RSC in 1960, and he developed Grotowski's ideals in his production of the *Marat Sade* by Peter Weiss in 1964.

Brook wrote his own theatrical philosophy in *The Empty Space* in 1968. He later stated:

these days I simply say to the lighting technician: 'Very bright!' I want everything to stand out clearly, without the slightest shadow ... I have not come to this conclusion through puritanism, nor do I want to condemn elaborate costumes or ban coloured lights. Only I've found that the true interest lies elsewhere.[59]

CONCLUSION

Perhaps the words of Peter Brook above are a suitable, sobering place to halt this exploration. Whilst neither a complete digest nor a comprehensive one, it is meant to illustrate the way that thinking has changed over the years, and the role of stage lighting developed.

This chapter also demonstrates how the diversity and flexibility of theatrical styles have grown and expanded to present us with a cornucopia of choices involved in the work we undertake as lighting designers.

Certainly there need no longer be set rules in anyone's mind concerning whether the lighting equipment can be seen or not, whether the houselights have to go out or not, whether the lighting has to be naturalistic, symbolic, expressionistic, surreal or any other such.

There is a multiplicity of choice in the theatre world that we now work within. A choice that allows each creative team a great freedom to explore ideas and develop them in any of a hundred ways. With this freedom also comes a responsibility to achieve something fine rather than something messily eclectic.

It does a lighting designer no harm at all to know something of the origins of the world they work in. It certainly helps in discussing abstract ideas with directors and the rest of the design team. On the other hand, it must be said, it is by no means essential either – a good instinct can still carry the day.

2 FIRST PRINCIPLES

INTRODUCTION – TOWARDS A DEFINITION

In theorizing about the practice of lighting for the stage, we shall discover how light is used as a tool; as a medium for expression. How the manipulation of even a single lighting source can help create mood or atmosphere. How the orchestration of a number of lighting sources becomes a powerful instrument with which to shape, elucidate, comment upon, and define the dramatic events unfolding on a stage.

Initially, let us attempt to define with some precision what it is that lighting on stage seeks to achieve, in essence, what lighting designed for the stage actually is. An accurate definition of what lighting encompasses, in this sense, will surely allow us to find our way more clearly as we contemplate and appraise the application of light on stage.

It is hoped that readers of this book have, on at least one occasion, been to a theatre performance of some kind, a performance that used stage lighting to carry out a number of functions – lighting used in a variety of ways.

Hopefully, you will also remember some of the following as being things you have actually seen lighting achieve – or maybe next time you go to the theatre you will identify some, if not all, of those listed below. (This without spoiling your enjoyment of the theatre occasion, of course). So:

Question:
What does stage lighting do?

Answer:
Successful stage lighting can do all of the following:

* *Illuminate* – Show an audience clearly what is on the stage, to 'project' the stage action towards the audience.
* *Separate* – Divide the action from the audience – and in so doing, further focus the attention of the audience away from themselves and on to the events on stage. Used as an aid to concentration – for example, this could be as basic as lowering the auditorium lighting at the beginning of a performance.
* *Embellish* – Decorate the setting of the action – to add to the scenery; for example, creating the effect of a full moon on a backcloth, or sunlight reflecting off water onto a nearby quayside.
* *Locate* – Reinforce the setting of the action – defining the time of day, the season, the weather, the locale, and so on.
* *Punctuate* – Demarcate the action on stage, that is, define scene breaks, delineate time intervals, change of location, and so on.
* *Pinpoint* – Draw attention to a particular part of the stage – that is, illuminate one part of the stage brighter than another, thereby drawing the audience's attention to appropriate action.
* *Disguise* – the opposite of the above – hide or make dark a stage event that the audience is not supposed to see or focus upon – for example, a scene change.
* *Create Mood* – Assist in the creation of the

mood of the drama – that is, help to give the stage events a dramatic context by reinforcing the dramatic atmosphere, this as distinct from the literal location of events provided by 'Locate' above.

✳ *Change Mood* – alter the dramatic moment – that is, increase or decrease the dramatic 'temperature' of a scene. Heighten or slacken the tension of the moment.

✳ *Create Spectacle* – create a dramatic moment in its own right – that is, the creation of wonder – often by use of special effects that stand on their own as dramatic events – for example, lightning, explosions, and so on.

Of course, stage lighting does not always achieve all of the above on every occasion. Different productions need different things – perhaps more illumination, less mood creation and certainly no spectacle, and so on. Nevertheless it seems to me that the ten concepts listed above are as close as we are going to get to defining the essence of theatre lighting.

Of course one can use any number of different terms to describe aspects of the list above. For example, we could have said that lighting *clarifies* what is on stage – that is, makes the dramatic intention clear. But this is surely implied in most of the examples listed which seek to make clear to the audience what the dramatic moment on stage is about.

Many of the categories also combine to create seemingly new ideas that one may be tempted to add to the list – for example, you could say that lighting can also *comment* on the stage picture by 'siding' with one element on stage rather than another – but if you look closely at the list above this would surely be a mixture of creating mood or changing mood, combined with 'pinpointing' – that is, 'pinpointed' mood. Generally speaking, I think these ten points will suffice and are worth studying. We will certainly need to refer back to them in what follows.

As a footnote to this introduction, it is interesting to note that people's opinions differ greatly as to which of the ten listed definitions of stage lighting is of the greatest importance. Although, of course, none can really stand alone – or at least rarely do so.

Visibility against mood is often the greatest debate. Many are overly fixated on spectacle to the cost of dramatic moment; some overly obsessed with verisimilitude at the cost of moving the action on or elucidating it more clearly.

Whatever the case may be, lighting should be there to help not to hinder – to allow the audience greater access to the drama not to act as a barrier to it – thus we should always be on our guard against overindulgence, obscurity, or unnecessary complexity.

In order to keep a clarity to our vision a useful expression to adopt should perhaps be that of the common artistic notion that 'less is more'. But what *less* and *more* are we talking about – what is our theorizing going to be actually about?

Our first principles must involve the basic nature of light itself and how to use it to illuminate the stage and the performers upon it.

THE NATURE OF LIGHT

In the wide band of electromagnetic waves (that is, from very short gamma rays to very long radio waves) the only waves visible to man occupy a narrow span from about 400–700nm (nanometers).

White light (daylight) is made up of an even amount of all the visible spectrum.

There are three factors involved in the perceiving of light: the light source, the object lit, and the eye.

An object is also dependent for colour upon the kind of light that strikes it. All objects, except light sources, are reflectors to some degree. Interestingly, a rough surface will reflect more light of all wavelengths than a smooth surface of the same colour. Thus, one appears brighter than the other.

A special kind of reflection phenomenon, called scattering, underlies the great expanses of colour in the sky or clouds – and explains the coloration of sunsets and sunrises. If there was nothing in the atmosphere – no dust or gases – the sky would appear black as in space. However when sunlight passes through the atmosphere, molecules of various gases scatter the light. Because they scatter the *short* wavelengths more (the blue end of the spectrum), the sky takes on a blue hue and the sun appears yellow.

When there is more dust or moisture in the air these particles act to scatter more of the *longer* wavelengths as well, and the sky becomes whiter – thus the white skies of a smog-laden city

The sun shining through a greater layer of the earth's atmosphere to reach us, as it has to do at sunrise or sunset, has to pierce an even greater degree of dust or moisture; the longer wavelengths are even more scattered than usual, and the sky appears more red or orange.

Various locations on earth give rise to particular local air conditions and thus a particular look to the sky – for example, the strong water content around Venice or Italy generally gives this area a famously luminous blue radiance.

One of the few, if only, benefits of air pollution can be said to be a greater preponderance of beautiful sunsets!

THEATRICAL LIGHT

In theatre terms, the first principle behind the most basic of requirements made upon theatre lighting is a straightforward one. Simply that if we shine a light upon an object it will become visible – we will see it.

If we examine this principle more carefully we immediately realize that this is more complex than it first appears. Basic questions arise

such as 'What light?' and 'How much light?' and more complex questions like 'What quality should the light have?' and 'What equipment shall we use?'

As detailed in the previous chapter, the history of lighting for the theatre sees a continual movement away from open air unlit performances towards the highly technical format with which we are familiar today. Namely, that in order to have total control of the visible medium – light – dramatic entertainment is (nearly always) performed in a windowless dark space. A space that, without the aid of specialized equipment, is in fact very dark indeed. Only low levels of safety light prevent it from being pitch-black.

In addition, we note that the light used to illuminate the stage attempts to be reasonably discreet and, for this as well as for creative reasons (as we shall discover), at some distance from the stage itself. In other words, light is projected to the stage from positions surrounding it.

However, in terms of visibility alone, an object is best lit from a position as close as possible to the viewpoint of the person observing it. Then all that is seen is also lit. But we only have to look at the two illustrations on page 26 to see that what is totally visible is not always as interesting as what is not.

In fact, the left-hand illustration displays perfectly an example of something that is considered in very derogatory terms in theatre lighting design: *flat lighting* – lighting that is 'flat' reveals a subject in such a way that it can be said to seem to have less 'character' or appear less 'interesting' than if lit in any other way.

Here we meet the first of the important principles that underpin theatre lighting design: *shadow is as important as light*. It is the interplay between light and dark that creates (amongst other things) visual interest. The great masters of the Renaissance period even had a word for this – they called it *chiaroscuro* (*see* page 12).

Flat lighting.

Angled lighting.

Flat lighting gives us total visibility but a rather poor picture. We could say that a stage picture that includes shade as well as light is more entertaining to the imagination, or that in such a case the brain is more stimulated.

Although shadow adds visual interest, total shadow – darkness – completely defeats the object of including any shading in the first place, by literally making an object unseeable.

Of course, this is also true of the amount of light we use. Use too much and we risk wiping out the visual interest we have created by swamping the stage picture. This happens either because in using too many different light sources we obliterate the shadows each source has created, or (even when using fewer sources) by using so much light that the shadows are lessened by the reflection or bounce coming from the over-bright sources.

What is required is that we strike a balance between light and dark. The lighting designer will ultimately spend quite a large amount of time dealing with this apparently simple aspect of the work. It may be expressed as a second principle thus: *a balance has to be found between visibility and interest.*

Naturally the finding of this important balance has to incorporate a decision about what is required of the lighting at any particular moment on stage. It will be different for each and every dramatic moment we seek to illuminate.

Making this decision about what a moment demands will itself require that we have the knowledge of what all the available lighting options are, and what each will communicate to an audience. Chapter 3 looks in some detail at these options as they involve a choice of lighting angles. Later chapters also look at dramatic intent on stage and how this inevitably motivates our decisions.

Before leaving the subject of light and dark, however, a few more basic concepts concerning visibility are worth discussing. These involve the question of how much of the stage picture do we actually have to illuminate to communicate the story of what is happening there? In the illustrations below we can see that only a part of a familiar object needs to be revealed for us to identify it. In other words, we can rely on the intelligence of the audience to assist in the basic of lighting roles – illumination to communicate the contents of the stage.

Using this factor it may be that we decide not to make visible a part of an object on stage. We may do this, of course, in two ways – either by casting shadows across it to create visual interest as we have already discussed, or by simply not lighting it in order to save equipment for use elsewhere.

In either case, the fact remains that we need not be overly obsessed with lighting everything. We can be selective. What we must strive for is to make sure that the audience understand what they are seeing. That what they see is lit in the way that is intended, and that this lighting is correct for that dramatic moment. Again this is all part of getting the right balance between light and dark, and visibility and interest.

It can also be seen that what we observe about an object is also true of a performer. In the illustrations at the top of page 28 we can tell the mood of the person from even a small part of their face. Although it does of course depend upon which part we are able to see!

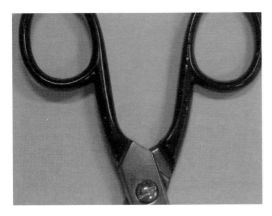

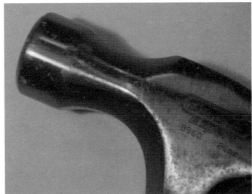

Recognition of everyday objects does not require that we see all of the object in question.

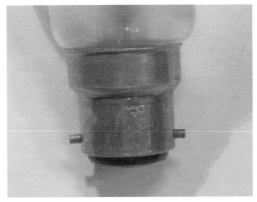

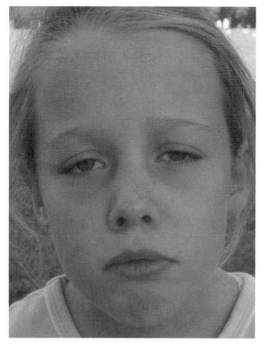

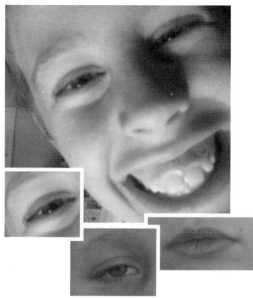

We only need to see part of the face to read the emotion.

A person's eyes are often referred to as 'the windows to the soul'. Thus it is most important that we see them, although not seeing them can have its own sinister implications! Likewise we should not underestimate how much easier it is to hear a person if we can see their lips. Lipreading plays a bigger part in the interpretation of meaning than many of us realize. Obviously of the two – eyes and mouth – the former, being deeper set in the face, offer a greater challenge to a lighting designer.

If visibility of the eyes is our priority it is important that we choose an angle of light shallow enough to light into the eye socket, and yet not too shallow as to open us up to the dreaded accusation of *flatness* in our lighting! (*See* page 29.) Once again a balance has to be found here, in this case dictated by a chosen requirement.

Another point to consider is that of *contrast*. This concerns the question of how much light is required on stage. Our eyes adjust to the level

of light around us. The iris that forms part of the eye opens and closes to allow only a certain amount of light through to our retina in order to send information about the images we perceive to the brain, but the eye can only work within a certain range – too much light and we are blinded, too little and we are straining to see. The iris contains muscles that vary the size of the pupil, the hole through which light enters the eye (*see* illustration below).

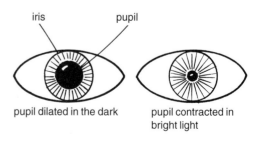

pupil dilated in the dark   pupil contracted in bright light

The human eye.

Face with eyes visible.

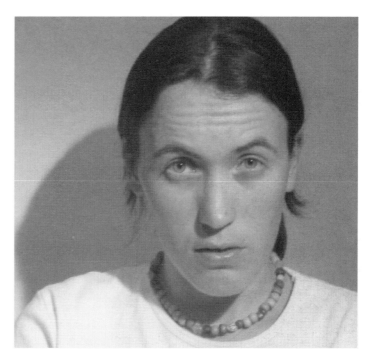

Eyes in shadow.

Light Relief

Contrast: A director is insistent that they are not getting enough light on stage – 'the laughs aren't big enough, it must be that the audience cannot see well enough'. The lighting designer is fast losing any hope of a visually interesting balance being maintained, the rig is nearly at full as it is. But not allowing himself to despair, the lighting designer asks for a moment to replot the lighting state. Plunges the stage into darkness, replots a few units that they feel have already got too bright at a slightly dimmer level, and then asks for the new, actually darker lighting state, to be made live on stage. The director, who has now been sitting in darkness for some time, looks at what seems to be a new and much brighter state, turns to the lighting designer and says 'thank you, that's much better' ...

Thus a certain light level on stage is required so that the audience are able to see an object at all. However, as already discussed, if there is too much light, we risk ruining our carefully crafted picture. Having established a balanced stage picture, however, it is important to realize that *contrast* plays a large part in how we would expect the audience to react to this picture.

A bright light source following on from a previously dark stage will make quite an impact (especially if brought on quickly – *see* Timings on page 60). The same bright source added to an already brightly lit stage may be almost imperceptible. Once again the notion of context becomes imperative. Each lighting state means something in its own right, but it also tells us different things depending where it is in the order of the stage narrative.

Lighting designers have been known, perhaps rather shamefully, to use the fact that contrast plays such a vital part in the way we perceive lighting to play a trick on overly pushy directors – as the anecdote to the right illustrates.

It is worth noting that as people find television to be more relaxing and less challenging than theatre performance, so it is that the eye and brain of an audience member find it easier, but perhaps less stimulating, to be given as much light as possible – that is, total visibility.

As lighting designers we want to give the audience the challenge of a more exciting vision and, as such, expect the audience to 'work' a little for their dramatic pleasure. The audience may be greedy to see with easy clarity totally everything presented on a stage; we, however, say to them – 'No, the intrigue is greater, the picture more attractive, if we hold some things back.' This understanding could be said to be part of the audience's contract with us when they buy a ticket to see a performance. The audience that observes the stage picture needs to want to see what we are going to show them – our role is to stimulate this interest and to hold it.

NB: There is a summary of this discussion at the end of the chapter.

In Practice

The Production of Light

Most central to all the work of a lighting designer is the instrument that produces the light. Properly referred to as a luminaire or, more often, a lantern.

Despite what manufacturers may try to tell us, in general terms the quality of light that comes out of any theatre lantern is very much the same, whatever the lantern. Light is light – it may be coloured, shaped, or made to move – but it still remains the thing we are familiar with in our everyday existence – visible, luminescent, illuminating, life-enhancing, light.

Modern lighting equipment uses as its source sophisticated light bulbs that are reliably bright,

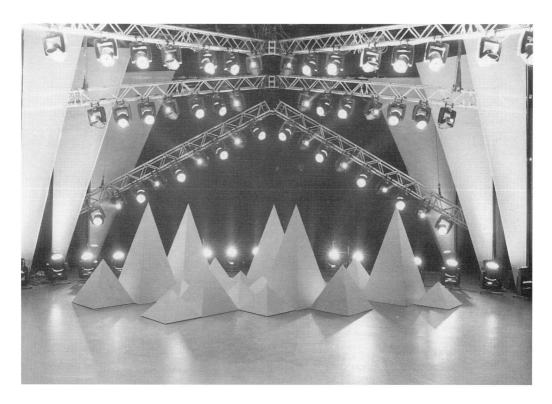

A full rig. The Vari*Lite demonstration Studio.

reasonably long-lasting (average lifetime of 700hr) and colour consistent. They comprise a tungsten filament, and an almost pure-quartz glass envelope, inside which is the inert gas halogen. They are usually described as quartz/halogen or tungsten/halogen bulbs.

The exceptions to this are lanterns that use a high-intensity discharge bulb. These use a spark between two electrodes to provide the intense light source they require, rather than a filament *(see* illustration overleaf).

In some cases so-called 'intelligent lights' also use discharge sources. Intelligent lights are lanterns that allow for remote control of many aspects of a normal unit. This includes being able to tilt and pan the unit itself, or redirect the light from it, also altering the focus,

shape, gobo, or colour. These expensive, but highly sophisticated units, are discussed towards the end of this chapter.

Apart from 'intelligent lights' there are many different lighting instruments available from many manufacturers, but what they all do is quite simple. In fact the differences between the basic units is not at all profound. All lanterns are designed to project light in one direction – usually, of course, we point this light towards the stage.

A manufacturer will make a range of lanterns, each unit in the range varying in the amount of power it uses, and thus the amount of light it produces. This distinction is generally realized (but not always) within a lantern by using bulbs of differing wattages.

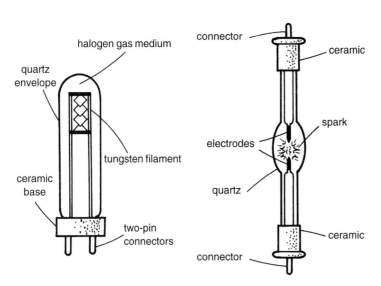

quartz envelope

halogen gas medium

ceramic base

tungsten filament

two-pin connectors

connector

ceramic

spark

electrodes

quartz

ceramic

connector

LEFT: The quartz halogen theatre bulb.
RIGHT: A discharge theatre bulb.

NB: In both cases, touching the quartz envelope discharges the bulb.

A basic unit will be designed to produce light that leaves it at a specific angle – that is, to produce light that will cover a certain area at any given distance. This is known as the unit's beam angle (*see* illustration on right).

The beam of light from a unit is generally brightest at its centre, it then falls away towards the edges. The point at which it falls below 50 per cent of the maximum output defines the beam angle. The point where it falls below 10 per cent is called the field angle.

Some units have an unalterable beam angle and are therefore referred to as 'fixed beam' units. Other units allow lenses to move, and by doing so create a range of possible beam angles – for example, the Strand unit, the SL 15/32, is so called as it produces beam angles over a range of 15 to 32 degrees.

Each manufacturer will, of course, claim that their lanterns produce more lumens (the usual measurement of light) for each watt of power than their rivals. In other words, that their instrument gives better value for money. This will depend on the quality of the optics within the unit. With many lanterns the precision of the optics (lens and reflector), as well as the efficiency of the bulb, become major selling points.

If you are purchasing or hiring equipment, these factors may well be of interest. Design

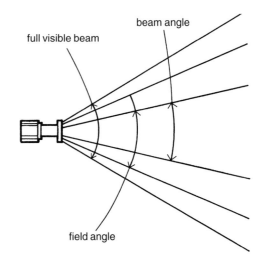

Lantern beam angles.

attractiveness, safety features, simplicity of use, lack of weight, and many other peripheral factors may also be considered important in the choosing of one unit over another.

However, when a lighting designer is given a list of equipment available in a venue, the important and relevant factors are different, as we shall see.

Lantern Types

Nearly all lanterns can be identified as belonging to one of five categories or types: flood, fresnel, profile, P.C. and beamlight.

The first of these, the flood, is a unit with no lens, the other four have different lenses and optical systems allowing them to perform variously different roles, and it is these variations that define them.

The chart overleaf describes each of these types, their usages, manufacturers' examples, special types within each category, and all the peripheral equipment associated with each type.

The five different types of lantern each have a particular role to play in stage lighting, and each is thus better at the thing it has been designed to do.

However, it is also important to note that the differences between the five basic lantern types are only really concerned with the following three factors:

1) The amount of light produced – how bright at its brightest?
2) The area the light covers – how big and/or small an area will it light? – That is, its *beam angle*.
3) The shaping of the light produced – does the unit produce a hard or soft-edged beam? Will it project a shape with accuracy (for example, a gobo)?

In a very competitive market, manufacturers are constantly trying to outdo each other and produce the best product at the best price. As with many products the cheapest units will, of course, not necessarily be the best. There are factors to be considered such as better light output; ease of use; robustness, available and economic spare parts and good after-service.

For example, in recent times the company ETC stole a march on its competitors by taking a serious leap forward in the optical effectiveness of the profile range. The 'source four' lantern produced a brighter, clearer and more efficient light for its 575watt bulb than any comparable 1,000watt unit. Eventually the other major manufacturers have produced their equally effective response – Strand's SL, CCT's Freedom and Selecon's Pacific ranges for example.

Light Relief

There are so many names given to equipment – manufacturers' sense of imagination often working overtime to come up with creative marketing ploys. Strand Lighting have only recently broken with their tradition of using musical terms – for example, Cantata, Coda, Quartet, Harmony, and so on. Their latest units have the amazingly imaginative prefix of SL.

But does it matter what things are called? Better to know what they do. Except that it does feel better saying 'Can you pass me the Patt 264?' rather than 'Can you pass me the banana-shaped lantern!'

On the other hand, we can over-mystify with our jargon. I have heard crew members taking the opportunity to put down a novice lighting designer who has asked for the right-hand shutter to be put in when focusing a Fresnel unit. 'No' they say 'it's a fresnel, it only has barndoors.' Whereas, in fact, little do they know that barndoor is simply a shortened form of 'Barndoor shutter'.

Lantern Type	Look of Beam	Typical Beam Angle	Focus	Peripherals	Special Types	Notes
Flood	Soft edged, large area	80–90 degrees	None	Gel frame/ barndoors	Cyc' floods	The only way to alter size is by moving the unit! Hence very inflexible, although as the name suggests, good for covering large areas. Cyc' floods often have linear bulbs, and the ability to throw light asymmetrically so that they can be rigged above or below a cyclorama.
Profile	Soft or hard edged	10–40 degrees	Hard OR soft focus of edges, shutters, gobo, etc.	Gel frame/ shutters/ iris/mask/ gobo/donut	Zoom, follow spot	Good optics allow for distance use, and good shaping and focusing of objects in beam, i.e. shutter or gobo. Also used in conjunction with motion effect wheels. Zoom versions allow more size flexibility. Often with Axial bulb mounting. May rarely be bi-focal, i.e. two focal planes.
Fresnel	Soft edged only, diffused	8–60 degrees	Large or small beam	Gel frame/ barndoors	NONE	Good controllable size feature – up to a large angle makes this a good partner to the more precise profile.
P.C.	Soft edged only, diffused	6–50 degrees	Large or small beam	Gel frame/ barndoors	NONE	Very similar to the fresnel but with better optics giving a greater light output and perhaps a slightly less diffused beam
Beam Light and Par	Soft edged	5–20 degrees	Small bright beam	Gel frame/ barndoors/ tophat/spill rings	Search light, follow spot	Specifically to make an intense tight beam. The par in its can (parcan) with its oval beam and fixed optics now dominates this field.

Lantern types.

34

In using the equipment described here it is important to emphasize the similarity between the lantern types as creators of beams of light as well as the differences.

When defining any piece of equipment (lanterns in particular) it is important to remain flexible when considering how it may be used.

Two examples:

1. It is worth noting that whilst a profile unit may be the brightest, most efficient way to light a soft-edged small area and to highlight a performer accurately, a fresnel that will also focus down to the same size may also do the job.
2. Usually the profile is used to project light from an out-front, above-the-audience position, in a proscenium theatre because it provides the better optics with which to do so; however, a similarly powered P.C. may also do just as good a job.

Intelligent Lights
Intelligent lights are also at heart simply producers of light, however, they allow us a greater flexibility. They fall into two basic types: moving head and moving mirror.

Moving Head
These units consist of an automated lantern – with motors to orientate and change direction of the entire unit and many other factors – colloquially I have heard them referred to as 'nodding buckets'. In some cases a motorized yoke can be fixed to a conventional unit thus converting it into a moving unit.

Moving Mirror
Perhaps less flexible in the context of theatre lighting, these units do as their name suggests – they project light onto a mirror that can be adjusted to reflect the beam wherever it is required. As the mirror weighs very little, these

Motorized yoke units from Selecon Lighting.

35

units have the advantage of being quieter than the moving head type.

The features of 'intelligent lights' differ from type to type but typically include: pan and tilt control, control of size and focus, colour changing, gobo changing, gobo spinning, the ability to add diffusion, to split and/or rotate a beam, to adjust shuttering, and so on.

Another important piece of equipment at the disposal of the lighting designer is the lighting control.

LIGHTING CONTROLS

The lighting control allows the lighting designer to designate specific output levels to any dimmer (and therefore the lanterns attached to it) and thereby create a 'lighting state'. It then allows for the accurate altering of this information over a period of time. A control 'board' can in fact be thought of as a remote-control device for the dimmers.

A 'lighting state' can be faded in or out over any preset timing. A straightforward swap, of one set of equipment for another, is called a 'cross-fade'.

The changing from one lighting state to another is defined as a cue. A play may contain any number of lighting states, and thus cues – typically more than one but usually less than 100. However, in a large and complex production – for example, a musical – there may be many more cues than this.

Manual Lighting Controls

A 'manual' lighting control requires that the level for a dimmer (and thus the lanterns attached to it) is set up by the operator on a single fader. A set of faders (one for each dimming channel) is called a 'preset'. A manual board will have at least two presets to allow for one lighting state to be live whilst another is being set up. It is unusual for a modern manual lighting board to have more than three presets.

Manual lighting boards – the LX series from Strand Lighting.

Cross-fades between states are also manually operated by means of a sliding control – (*see* illustration above).

Modern manual lighting boards also incorporate some of the computer technology described below – perhaps most notably the means to operate cross-fades between presets by a prescribed pre-plotted time.

Memory Lighting Controls

A typical memory lighting control uses computer technology to set and remember levels, run and repeat cues at set timings, and so on. A 'memory board' thus allows for fast changing and yet deadly accurate reproduction of cues. Many modern lighting boards will also run effects – that is, chases, lightning, fire flicker and disco effects – as well as control intelligent lighting units.

The control board may also have its own remote control so that lanterns can be made live; plotted into lighting states; the show run; all from positions other than at the console of the main board.

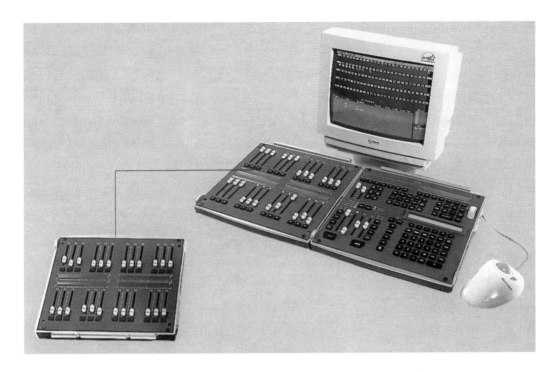

A computer lighting board – the 300 series from Strand Lighting.

Lighting controls are made by a number of manufacturers who all have their specific layouts. Obviously the type of lighting control required for any given production or venue is dictated by the use required of it.

At first glance a memory board may seem far superior to a manually operated machine, but in fact in a venue that receives different productions every day – perhaps in a cabaret style – the ability to alter plotted cues manually as a show progresses cannot be overvalued, neither can the simplicity of a board that a touring technician has to learn in half an hour. For this very reason even the most sophisticated of memory lighting boards often have a manual 'wing', and hybrid boards exist that are as much 'manual' as 'memory'.

In a similar vein, a production that uses 'intelligent lights' may choose to control them from a separate lighting control and thus run two lighting boards with two operators. In some cases, the pre-production may be a lot easier with two controls. Once the lighting has been set, the information is then downloaded to a smaller control for 'playback' in performance.

Lighting control boards can appear very daunting, but the thing to remember is that they are manufactured to aid the process not hinder it. Also that what each machine can do, is not only generally similar from type to type, it is also what one would expect and hope it would do – that is, store information, replay it, take timings, allow individual channels to be raised and lowered, and so on.

NB: The manner in which the lighting control board contributes to the lighting of a theatre is discussed on pages 60–1.

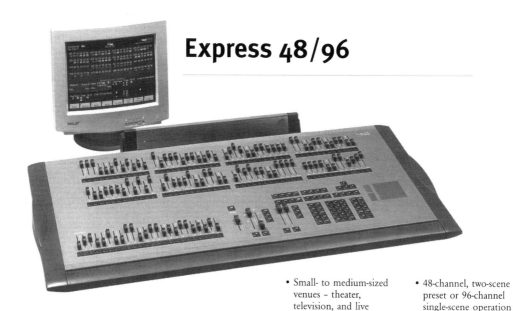

Express 48/96

- Small- to medium-sized venues – theater, television, and live concerts
- 144 channels **NEW**
- 48-channel, two-scene preset or 96-channel single-scene operation
- Comprehensive moving light control package

A hybrid lighting board – with good manual and computer capacities – the Express 48/96 from ETC.

CONCLUSION

It is just as important to remain flexible in our thinking in the area of light usage as it is in the instruments that produce and control it. As I have already stated, in general terms, all lanterns are simply devices that allow us to project light to where we want it. Whilst some lanterns are obviously better at some things than others, we should be careful not to overdefine their usage or we may well miss opportunities to use the equipment at our disposal to its maximum potential. The same is true of the many variations of lighting controls and indeed light itself.

Chapter Summary

- Total visibility is visually boring.
- Interplay between light and shadow creates visual interest.
- A balance must be struck between clarity and character.
- In lighting selectively a clear judgement is required as to what is dramatically appropriate.

3 LIGHT REVEALING FORM

How light falls onto an object affects what we see of it. Even more significantly perhaps it may also influence how we *feel* about the object.

SOURCES OF LIGHT

We have already seen how lighting an object from the point of view of the observer creates a flat or, to be more emotive, boring picture. Also that a single beam of light can, if striking an object from a more oblique angle, create a very attractive image. Nevertheless, although dra-

matic, a single beam of light used in this way is very artificial. Because it is not what we are used to seeing in the world around us.

Light originating from the sun can be thought of as emanating from a single light source. However, by the time the sunlight illuminates the things around us, it has become diffused and scattered. This happens to the light and to differing degrees, due to the effect of the earth's atmosphere, and other prevailing local climatic and geographical conditions, as the light journeys from the sun to the earth.

Even on the sunniest of days, when the sun sits in a clear blue sky, the strong and obvious shadows that the sunlight creates are not pitch-black (*see* illustration below).

Shape in light.

Light and shade on a sunny day.

In order to light an object in our dark theatre as we would see it in daylight – thus to give it some sense of the norm – we need to use two sources. One to create the direct original source of light (the sun), the other to replicate the other diffused light we are used to seeing.

This also applies to the replicating of other sources:

Moonlight obviously acts in a very similar way to sunlight – moonlight is simply reflected sunlight after all.

Artificial light is also usually seen in confined spaces and therefore reflects and diffuses – for example, room lighting inside a house. Or it is deliberately diffused to create a good working light – for example, street lighting, fluorescent light.

The brightest of these two necessary sources is known as the *key light*. In photographic parlance, in particular, the other source is known as *fill light*.

NB: In theatre terminology a 'fill light' can also mean a low-level source, filling in any unfortunate unwanted shadows in an other-wise finished lighting state. To prevent confusion, this usage is avoided in this book!

Photographers, and cinematographers for that matter, have the advantage of lighting for the camera, a directional device that only sees what they want it to, and so they often use gadgets to bounce the light from the key source back to the object, thus creating a fill light much as it occurs in the real world. This something that on stage we rarely have the opportunity to do.

Key light is the brightest, most obvious source of light hitting an object and as such, therefore, the fill light must be at a considerably lower level.

Naturally if the key light and the fill light are at the same or similar level then we run the risk of once again creating flat lighting (*see* illustration below right).

Again the requisite word here is *balance*. Obviously in this case we are greatly mistaken if we think that by balance we mean that both sides should be equal.

Another principle can be stated at this point, and sums up what we have found so far:

Object lit with directional light.

Object lit with no key – flat.

key and fill light create both interest and the familiar.

A bright keyed light source creates interest, as we have previously noted, by lighting an object to create chiaroscuro – a stimulating interplay between light and dark (*see* page 25). It is the fill light that provides us with the familiar, the usual. Giving us credibility by providing the diffused light source that we associate with everyday situations, and that is usually lacking in the artificial black box of a theatre space.

Using two sources in this way furnishes us with the starting point of the norm. We can then depart from this point of authenticity to varying degrees, deciding whether we wish to be more or less dramatic or realistic.

The credibility of these two light sources is particularly enhanced when the key light comes from an expected quarter. Typically from somewhere *above* the object, as would the sun or other normal light source.

This in turn is made more recognizably believable if the key light comes from an angle other than that at right angles to the observer. Obviously, there are occasions in the real world when we happen to be standing in such a way that sunlight is hitting those things around us from one of the four positions at right angles to the object. However all the other less symmetrical angles

Objects lit with directional light, which results in good key creating depth and character.

available round an object are much more likely – that is, with a one-in-ninety chance of hitting a right angle, the world is seldom that orderly!

Oblique angles of light – that is light from asymmetrical angles at some remove from the viewpoint of the observer – create more than just interest and a visual sense of the everyday.

If we understand that the non-oblique angles create lighting described as flat, this is because in making an object appear shadowless it actually does look flat. Then we must realize that oblique angles of light create the opposite effect: *oblique angles of light create a sense of depth.*

NB: If we use angles that are particularly oblique then the tendency is that depth is exaggerated. This is because the shadows cast by even the slightest of texture on an object are greater than we would normally expect.

In Practice

In making use of our understanding of lighting form, the expectancy of the audience is once again to the fore. The audience is not expecting to see an object, apparently placed within a recognizably normal context, lit in an extreme manner – in such a case they are more likely to believe that the object itself is of greater depth rather than that the lighting is causing the effect.

For this reason exaggerated angles have the effect of projecting an object towards the viewer. This is very useful when the audience may be viewing the drama from some distance away, or where there is a likelihood that the actors may blend into the background.

Using exaggerated or highlighted angles in this way becomes to the lighting designer a device similar to that of the actor 'projecting' his voice in a large auditorium. The actor, whilst in the most intimate and quiet of scenes, nevertheless speaks artificially loudly, and yet without seeming to. The drama is projected

ABOVE: An object flatly lit blends into the background.
BELOW: An object with key light stands out from the background.

The setting brought to life with light – Sleeping Beauty *(Polka Theatre).*

clearly to the audience who do not notice the artifice being used to do so.

Viewed from some distance away, the human frame does appear somewhat slight – and so these oblique, exaggerated angles of light that project a performer forward, are of great us in all forms of staged event (*see* illustration above). This is not to forget that these oblique angles are also of use when lighting scenery, and once again particularly in the context of large auditoria. Light from such angles skimming a scenic structure can help amplify the smallest of details. The notion of texture on an object is thus conveyed to the distant observer, and that object is brought vividly to life before them.

LIGHTING ANGLES

Back-Light

Perhaps the most oblique of angles, and the most exaggerated of key lights is light that originates from behind an object.

Used in isolation, back-light creates silhouette. Silhouette is a striking feature in its own right, and often used as such on stage. In such cases although the object's darkened side faces the audience, nevertheless its mere outline can still communicate a surprising amount of information (*see* illustration below).

Used in combination with other sources, and especially as the key source, back-light produces a halo around an object. In just showing the edge of an object it is also often referred to as 'rim light'.

Like other oblique sources of light often used as key lights, back-light promotes the idea of dimensionality, the reality, or the depth of an object. This is particularly the case against dark backgrounds or backgrounds of the same colour as an object in question (*see* illustration page 45, top)

As with other key sources an 'off-centre' back-light lends itself to the better creation of verisimilitude, or naturalness, in a stage picture. The so-called three-quarter back-light source that glances over the 'shoulder' of an object is very popular for just this reason.

Side-Light

Another form of rim light is produced from lighting sources placed at the side of an object or performer.

Hiawatha *(Torch Theatre Co.).*

The actor on the right disappears against the black background – Measure for Measure *(Rada).*

Actors lit with rim light stand out from the background – Mowgli's Jungle *(Rada – lighting by Julia Pollit).*

45

Side-light – Camino Real (Rada – lighting by David Bishop).

Side-lighting can appear most striking. It is particularly popular for lighting dance. Unlike sources of light coming from above a performer, side-light does not favour the head or face. Instead the full figure of the dancer is lit with an equal worth placed along the full height of the body. For dance this is often realized by placing side-lighting

at a number of heights alongside the stage – and it's not for nothing that lower positions are known colloquially as 'shin-busters'.

Angles of light from above the acting area favour the top of the performer (the head and face) in two ways:

1. The light hits the top of the performer first and thus any shadows cast go down onto the body. The head is thus better lit.

2.

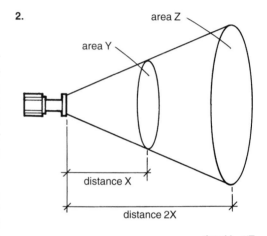

area Z

area Y

distance X

distance 2X

thus Y = ¼Z

1.

light source

height a = 2b
area y = 4w
In doubling the height of a cone, the area of the base is multiplied by a factor of 4.

a

b

y

w

The trigonometry of beam angles.

3.

light source

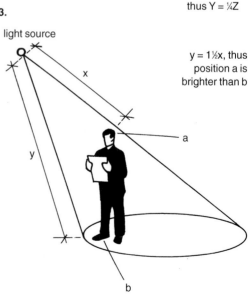

y = 1½x, thus position a is brighter than b

x

a

y

b

Low-angled light in use –
Measure for Measure
(Rada).

2. The nearer an object is to the source, the brighter the light hitting it compared with things further away. An object twice as far away from a source is a quarter as brightly lit (*see* diagram). Thus the head

Side-light.

being nearer to the source is also brighter than the body.

It is worth noting in passing that, combined with an appropriate apparent locale and colour, side-light is also useful in conveying the concept of the sun setting or rising – as only at dawn or dusk do we expect to see the sun at such specifically low angles.

Cross-Light

This angle also comes from the side of the action or performer – in this case differing from pure side-light in being from the side *and above* the performer. As such it provides much of the effective look of side-light but from a more generally 'naturalistic' angle.

Cross-light can be thought of as a softer, that is, less dramatic, angle than that of side-light. It is particularly useful when the need is for side-light but no positions to the side of the stage area are available. Obviously cross-light is not so 'even handed' on the overall figure of a performer as is side-light, and therefore less often used for dance. Cross-light can often be a little too shadowy and unclear for really effective illumination of the face of the performer.

47

Up-Light

As its name suggests, this is illumination from a source below an object, and it creates the most unreal of appearances. It is the angle of light that we are most unfamiliar with in our everyday life. This is particularly true when it is used to light the face, where, for example, we see nose and eyebrow shadows thrown upwards giving a weird, strange and even horrific look.

For this reason up-light has been widely used, on stage and in film alike, to portray the macabre and villainous. This trend continues today where, even in futuristic dramas, many a 'bad guy' is effectively uplit by computer screen or console.

Historical note: it is interesting to note that during the days of candle and gaslight (that is, prior to the invention of projected light) it was imperative to get the light source as close as

*ABOVE: **Cross-light.***
*BELOW: **Up-light in use in Brecht's** Man Equals Man (Contact Theatre Co.).*

Light Relief

Expectation: I have tried this on many students new to ideas of lighting and it seldom fails to work.

In a darkened studio I set up a number of lighting positions pointed at a single person – usually seated. We look at each source individually first and I ask the group to comment on what the source 'says' to them. Usually a bright up-light source is greeted with the best response. The students have no trouble in describing it 'macabre', 'suggesting horror', 'weird'. I then ask them if in any way that source of light could ever be used to suggest an idea of comfort, contentment, peace. Having looked at the source for some while, they always say an emphatic 'No' in reply to this.

I then lower the level of the unit to a warmer glow, and continually flickering it slightly, say 'now imagine you are home from a cold day's work outdoors, in your favourite armchair, at last in front of a gently warming fire.'

Suddenly the up-light takes on a whole new and yet totally convincing aura, proving once again that context is everything!

possible to the stage. For this reason foot-lighting was particularly favoured. Thus, for generations, the appearance of staged productions was the same whatever the drama, with up-light in the form of foot-lighting generally predominant. It must have been viewed (literally) as just the way the stage world happened to look, and as such never questioned.

Check the index for further references to foot-lighting, as throughout the history of theatre lighting everyone seems to have had an opinion on it. Even in the modern age, the habit

front elevation

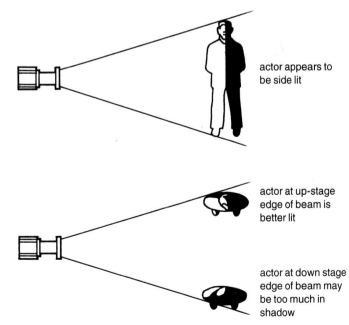

actor appears to be side lit

in plan

actor at up-stage edge of beam is better lit

actor at down stage edge of beam may be too much in shadow

Problems with side-light.

of foot-lighting took a while to break, and in many people's minds is still associated with the thespian world.

Today, therefore, up-lighting has a role in suggesting the macabre or strange, a period performance, or a strong sense of the theatrical.

USING ANGLES

It must be remembered that when applying the theory of lighting angles, we are dealing with units that produce cones of light not neat lines, and as such actors can end up being more in shadow than intended – that is, behind the light source rather than in front of it (*see* illustration below).

CONCLUSION

In looking at the way sources of light from different positions work, we soon begin to realize

that the wide variety of angles available to us make very different comments. In this chapter we have tended to look at only the most extreme examples, obviously less excessive variations are available between them.

Much of the time a sense of 'naturalism' has governed our ideas, as we inevitably look to judge lighting from a perspective of the familiar. But a sense of the 'emotional value' of a source of light is also clearly available.

It is always important to know where we are diverging from the norm, and what we expect the audience's reaction to be to what we create before them. Their expectation informs and should be reflected in our work as lighting designers.

The lit performer – **Attempts on Her Life** *(Rada – lighting by David Bishop).*

Chapter Summary

- Light gives form to volume.
- Oblique, angled light best conveys depth.
- Oblique angles promote and project volume and show texture.
- Sunlight diffuses – to recreate it on stage at least two sources are required.
- A single strong source amongst several creates key light.
- A weaker source of light can be called fill light.
- Key light from high, off-centre sources is most visually acceptable because it is more naturalistic.
- Rim light (back-light) displays shape or form particularly well.
- An object could be described as best lit with three sources – providing key, fill and rim light.
- Rim light from the side (side-light) displays form well and evenly in the vertical plane.
- Up-light is the most alien of sources.
- Audience expectation can transcend even the strongest of intentions.

4 COMMUNICATING WITH SHAPE

In the last chapter we found that an object, although in silhouette, will still clearly convey a great deal of visual information. An outline alone can often tell us what an object is, and therefore what we are looking at.

As such, rim light (often as back-light) can be said to have a specific role to play in promoting dimensionality. It does this by concentrating the eye on the silhouette of an object.

Shaped light can also direct messages to an audience in other ways:

THE SHAPING OF LIGHT

Light projected onto a stage inherently has to be of some shape. The edges of the beam may be clearly visible or vaguely defined – described as hard or soft. The hardness or softness of the beam depends on the equipment in use and how it is focused to project light (*see* table on page 34).

Hard- and soft-edged beams can be used in ways that an audience will not be expected to

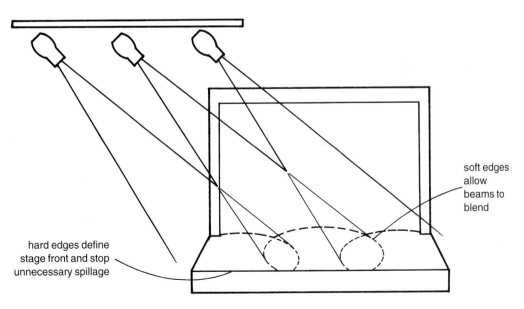

soft edges allow beams to blend

hard edges define stage front and stop unnecessary spillage

Typical unseen use of soft and hard beam edges.

notice. A hard edge may be used to trim the edge of a beam of light that would otherwise fall into the audience – for example, on the front edge of a stage. Soft edges may be used to allow the light from one lantern to blend seamlessly with that from another (*see* illustration on page 51).

In these cases the shape of the edge of the beam of light becomes merely functional, not seeking to communicate anything to the audience.

Where hard and soft edges are made deliberately visible to an audience, often delineating an area or individual on stage, the general point can be made that *hard edges are aggressive and soft edges are passive*.

Depending as always on the dramatic context, hard edges read as conveying interrogation, angst, anger, psychological stress, inner turmoil. Conversely, the soft edges impart calm, happiness, inner peace, warmth, and so on.

However we must be careful with these distinctions, since in some contexts they become irrelevant. For example a follow-spot may be used in a pantomime, and in such a case the hard edge of the beam will not be seen to detract one iota from the hilarity of the moment, simply conveying what has become understood as a theatrical device in use.

Soft edges blend in so well with their surroundings, and are not generally disconcerting to the eye; as such they are also useful if no dramatic comment is required at all.

Concepts of hard and soft as aggressive and passive can be seen to be generally true, but the degree of their effect is extremely relative. As we have already discussed, in some dramatic contexts where other influences are much stronger, they can seem not to apply at all. In some cases the shaping of light may also be recognized as specific to the location or event in hand rather than promoting a mood in its own right. Once again context becomes paramount.

In Practice

The vast majority of lanterns, left unhindered by any functional device, project a circular beam that, when projected onto the stage from anywhere (other than the vertical), fall as an ellipse.

NB: Profile units use shutters and can be focused to produce hard or soft edges – other equipment produces only soft edges to the light it produces. As noted in the previous chapter par units are unusual in that they produce an oval beam.

An example: imagine a summer harvest scene with, as part of it, sunlight broken into sharp rectangular shapes as it streams through a slatted fence. This would not, in the context of a sunnily lit state, read as aggressive. An audience would simply accept it as the expected occurrence in the location being portrayed.

However, it is to be noted that the set and lighting designer of this peaceful scene had, as is always the case, a choice – the fence and the lighting through it need not have been designed to appear as aggressive at all. Perhaps there was an ulterior motive. Let us revisit the scene.

The peaceful harvest scene is interrupted by the arrival of a bullying rival team of workers – an individual is picked on and thrown to the ground. Where he lands his face is suddenly dramatically emphasized – he has landed in such a way that the brutally cut light through the fence now crosses his bewildered and disquieted face. It is dramatically effective, and yet the shaped light is perfectly in context.

It is important to understand that as part of our lighting design we need to manipulate the context of the piece on which we are working to provide us with dramatic emphasis in just the manner of the example above. It is something that we will return to in Chapter 7 when discussing the creation of mood.

The appeal of pattern in nature.

It is also interesting to note that as a general rule the human eye and brain are particularly attracted to repeated designs and, as with the slatted fence imagined in our example above, this often occurs as a lengthy light/dark/light repetition

Evidence for this is all around us – from fabric and wallpaper designs, to great works of art (literal and abstract). Also it can be seen in the natural way sunlight falls upon objects or in the objects themselves.

This is something we can use on stage to our advantage to enhance the picture we are lighting. A common example is the lighting of stage stairways. They particularly appeal when the light comes from above or behind – each level tread is then clearly lit with the riser in dark relief between them.

Light can also be projected onto the stage in very specific shapes – shapes that create precise impressions in the minds of the audience.

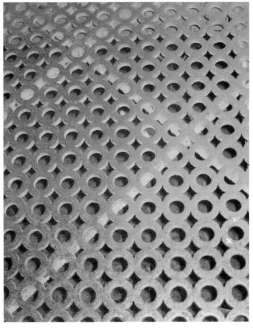

Man-made patterning.

Natural light on steps – the appeal of repeated patterns.

Natural gobos.

Symbols, words, signs, even pictures can be projected – usually using devices that are known as gobos. As the illustration below shows, some of these shapes can be very exotic, and are perhaps less likely to be of regular use.

ABOVE AND ABOVE RIGHT: Gobos.
BELOW AND BELOW RIGHT: Gobos – the more useful range.

More useful are projections that display light as we are more likely to see it: through windows or trees, light representing stars or the moon (*see* illustrations on page 55 and opposite). Often these are a particularly good way to convey to an audience evidence of things that the set design or pace of the production cannot afford to create in any more substantial way.

For example in a play of many short scenes it may be too cumbersome to change the set for each moment – some of the works of Shakespeare come to mind. Thus a subtly placed beam representing a castle window may well suffice, doing away with the need for any large set structure to be brought on stage. The same is obviously true of the effect of beams suggesting light through trees – very commonly used as an effective way to substitute for the trees themselves and yet very evocative.

Light Relief

I have worked many times with the distinguished director William Gaskill – one of the founding fathers of the English Stage Company at the Royal Court, and director of many seminal works of the late twentieth century, for example Bond's *Saved*.

When talking about lighting, Bill often states that he wants 'no colour' and 'no gobos' in a production.

'No gobos' is quite a general comment from directors – especially of a certain generation. I tell my students that they must have been frightened at an early age by the misuse of a gobo. I imagine one brandished recklessly under the nose of a baby director in a cot!

More likely I think the unsubtle use of gobos has put them off for life. It is no good if you are watching a piece of theatre, being wonderfully enticed by the atmosphere of the piece, when a hard focused shape suddenly looms at you simply shouting 'device'.

On one occasion I was working on a production of *Electra* with William Gaskill and his co-director/designer Henk Schut. A couple of my ideas for the overall concept behind the lighting had been rejected, and I was wondering how next to proceed when I wandered into rehearsals one day just as they were breaking up for lunch. 'Any ideas about the lighting yet?' I asked. 'You know', said Bill, 'I rather like what we have here already.' They were rehearsing on set in the studio that was our venue. It was dark and shadowy with only a few functioning working lights – sun floods. It was an interesting atmosphere but in places almost totally in darkness. For a short while I actually thought I had found the lighting designer's holy grail – no rig, no focusing, no plotting – simply take the fee and run.

A few days later I plucked up courage to ask Bill if he really meant no rig – 'Of course not', he said, 'I do need to see them! I just want it to look as if we haven't put up a rig!' This is of course easier said than done. So duly a rig went up. The original working lights had in many cases shone through the lighting bars – and so I had units placed above the rig to cast similar shadows. Where I could not find a similar position I had used gobos.

During the lighting rehearsal Bill looked at one such shadow crossing the back brick wall of the studio (There was hardly any set) – 'Is this a gobo?' he asked. I thought I would hedge my bets. 'Does it look like one?' I rejoined. 'Well, if it is, it's a damn good one', he said with a twinkle in his eye, and walked away. The gobo stayed.

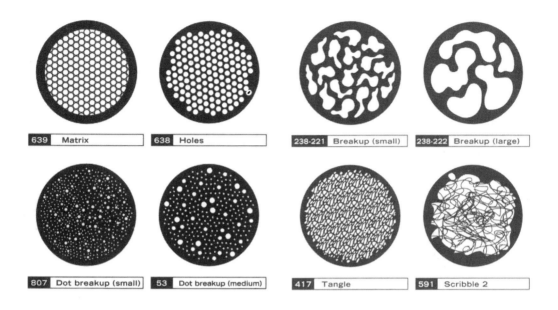

| 639 | Matrix | 638 | Holes | 238-221 | Breakup (small) | 238-222 | Breakup (large) |

| 807 | Dot breakup (small) | 53 | Dot breakup (medium) | 417 | Tangle | 591 | Scribble 2 |

*ABOVE AND BELOW LEFT: **Gobo break-ups.***

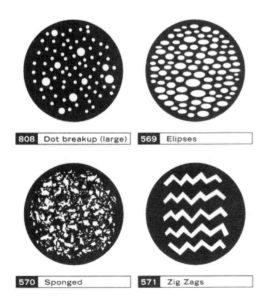

| 808 | Dot breakup (large) | 569 | Elipses |

| 570 | Sponged | 571 | Zig Zags |

Gobos in use – Guys and Dolls (Rada – lighting by Andrew Turner).

57

More useful again are softly diffused shapes that break the light up, adding character to it without the limitation of describing anything specific.

In this case the break-up of light could be described as adding texture to light, making a unique contribution to a stage picture.

CONCLUSION

In this chapter we have seen that shaped light communicates information of many kinds to an audience. Acknowledging that shaped light can sometimes be very exact, hard-edged and specific, nevertheless perhaps the less obvious, softly focused shapes are, in their subtle way, the more powerful and sophisticated tool.

Chapter Summary

- Shape conveys information.
- Hard- and soft-edged beams may be merely functional.
- Hard-edged beams may be thought of as aggressive.
- Soft-edged beams may be thought of as passive.
- The edges of soft-edged beams are often imperceptible.
- Repetition of shape appeals to the eye.
- Context can dictate the way shape is perceived.
- Shape may add to context by suggestion.

Light defining space – Fanfare (Rada – lighting by Sebastian Barraclough and David Bishop).

5 THE FASCINATION OF MOVEMENT

Light in motion on a stage can either be real or suggested. In either case, it can also be most bewitching. The allure of such movement can thus prove to be a very powerful theatrical device.

REAL MOVEMENT

Shaped light on stage can benefit greatly from the addition of movement. Light beams shaped (and coloured) to represent light reflecting from water or emanating from fire, for example, remain merely symbolic unless we can see them appearing to ripple or flicker. The resul-

tant effect can add both verisimilitude and visual interest to an appropriate scene – its contribution helping to keep the stage alive both physically and dramatically.

Movement of this kind fascinates. Who has failed to be entranced by the lively flames or last dying embers of a winter fire, the gently trickling movement of a stream, the crashing of breakers on a beach, driving rain on a car windscreen, or the scurrying motion of windswept clouds crossing an open sky?

In fact if we choose to recreate these elemental features on stage we must take care not

Light and movement.

to distract from the action with the persuasive and often mesmerizing quality of the moving images portrayed.

We can however use these suggested natural elements on stage to further enhance the dramatic mood. In the literary world this conceit is called synaesthesia – the natural elements reflecting the atmosphere of the text, as in 'It was a dark and stormy night ...'. These very literal moving images have a particular role in a stage production. Often they will be specified by the script or set design but, because of their very literal nature, there may not be a role for them in a production at all.

The use of these special effects in lighting is often one of temptation versus sensibility. They can easily be overused and badly applied. However, they do have their place and, if used well, can create and enhance wondrous and spectacular theatrical moments.

SUGGESTED MOVEMENT

A more common type of movement in light is the fade or cross-fade – that is, the movement from one light state to another as a cue (*see* Lighting Controls on pages 36–8).

A cue may dictate any number of complexities of cross-fade. It may be that a single lantern is exchanged for another, or a whole complex lighting state replaced with another, a sequence of cross-fades run one after another, or a much smaller subtle alteration made to a stage picture. It may also be the case that light is coming on from near dark or dying down to black – that is, a fade rather than a cross-fade.

The particular context dictates which of these is relevant – the choice being the one that is needed to progress the action as the director, designer and/or lighting designer feels that a piece in hand requires.

Whether manually or computer-operated the change or movement of lighting has to occur over a certain time period. As such a cue

is 'given' a timing that remains the same each time it is run in its appointed place in the action.

The duration of the cross-fade may be instantaneous (a snap or cut cue), slower (average cross-fades are typically 3–10s) or much, much slower (typically 10–20min or longer).

Fast cues can be considered aggressive and eye-catching, whilst slower cues are passive, gentle, and may, on occasion, be imperceptible.

THE TIMING OF CUES

The following table shows that way that one would normally expect timings to be perceived in most dramatic contexts:

Timing of Cue	Effect
Snap	Very eye-catching/dramatic/aggressive
1–2s	Eye-catching/harsh
3–5s	Fast/pacey but not too harsh
6–10s	Normal acceptable change/undramatic
11–40s	Gentle but visible change
41s – several min	Probably imperceptible change/subliminal

Light Relief

Even in the age of gaslight, the nineteenth-century actor-manager William Macready was well aware of the power of lighting, and the use of subtle cues.

A critic once wrote of his performance: 'When Mr Macready comes on stage it is as if the whole world lights up'.

In fact, whatever the play, on Macready's first entrance stage hands were instructed to increase gently the supply of gas to the lighting in the theatre!

Of course these are only rough guides. It is, for example, quite possible for a snap cue to appear both dramatic and imperceptible! By which I mean that even a large dramatic change of lighting can be 'imperceptible' in the sense that it so suits the moment that it goes by unnoticed by the audience.

A cue placed on the exact moment of a stage explosion, a shout, or strong gesture may be just such a case – if 'right' the audience will hardly notice it, and will certainly not question the validity of the movement.

One has only to see such a cue misplaced, half a second before or after the correct moment, to notice it can also be tonally and joltingly interruptive to a production. Such heart-rending moments (for the lighting designer in particular) – when the lighting operator or stage manager cueing the production gets it wrong or the lighting designer themselves have set the wrong timing – only show what underlying power such changes contribute to the drama when properly placed.

Note also that the manner in which a lighting rig reacts to dimmers, how many units are changing in level and over what range, and what the stage action consists of during the change, will all, amongst other factors, have a big effect on the choice of appropriate timing. The dramatic requirement of a particular moment will, of course, also affect the decision enormously. It can take time to get these aspects right, and the lighting designer will usually refine timings continually throughout the technical rehearsal period.

SPLIT TIMINGS

A single cue can also have two timings – the first dictating lanterns rising in output (including coming on from being off) is called the 'up time'. The second controlling lanterns dimming out (or going off altogether) is called the 'down time'. Both up and down timings on a single cue can be set at the same level – that is, a pure cross-fade – or at different levels. By 'splitting' the timing in this way, various effects are created.

A split cue with a faster up time means a new lighting event will arrive before the old one has departed – helping to speed along the action, and preventing any unfortunate dip in the stage picture as a result of the cross-fade.

A split cue with a faster down time will usually create a dip in the stage picture, usually at approximately the half-way point of the cue. This may be useful to punctuate the action, possibly mark the passage of time, or a shift in locale or the dramatic mood. It may also be thought of as giving the audience time to reflect.

CROSS-FADE MOVEMENT

The timing of a cue is only one aspect of the manner in which a sense of movement is involved in a cross-fade. The cross-fade itself can appear to move light from one place to another – changing emphasis and locale. It can result in a shift in mood or in dramatic atmosphere. The lighting may appear to shrink around a person or thing. This is called 'closing-down' and gives an effect not unlike that of the 'close-up' in cinematic terms. Conversely the light can appear to 'open-out', to expand – in cinema terms to pull away from the object.

In these cases we are talking about using light to focus or defocus our attention to a specific point or event on stage, as well as change the mood or atmosphere of the piece. Obviously the timing of such cues, the movement of lighting states, can be seen to have quite an influence on how the audience perceives the stage picture.

To emphasize this point, here is a commonly used device or trick of the trade, involving the movement of light and the timing of a cue.

It is often the case that to create an appropriate atmosphere for a doom-laden or eerie piece of theatre, the lighting has to be really quite dark. At the same time, this lighting state may be too dark for the audience to see the actors clearly, without incurring eye strain. In such cases it is common to establish the initial mood with the dark lighting state and then, once the action has begun, to imperceptibly creep up the lighting level, the better to illuminate the performers.

Such cases have slow timings, but even if they are 'obvious' to the viewer it is hoped that they give the same effect as you would expect when walking into a dark room – that is, your eyes adjust to the new level so that eventually you see more clearly in the gloom, thus using our everyday experience to justify a necessary cue.

IN PRACTICE

Animation devices and special lighting effects units of one kind or another are commonly used to create real movement in light. In fact by definition a lighting 'special effect' is a unit that produces light on stage that moves in some way.

These units may be roughly grouped into two categories: those devices that add on to a standard lighting unit (for example on to a profile or fresnel); these I have called 'Attachment Effects'. Secondly, devices that are made to create an effect and have their own light source; these I have labelled as 'Special Effect Units'.

In most cases, the special effect unit is one that has been designed to provide a solution for the needs of a stage production. Not surprisingly, the effect of flickering light emanating from a fire, or light reflecting from moving water are very common examples, and both feature very strongly in the list that is about to follow.

'Intelligent lights' can also produce some good moving light effects, many of which are similar to those produced by a number of the special effects units described in this chapter.

What follows is a list of the most commonly used effects.

Attachment Effects

Gobo Rotator

The insertion of a gobo into a lantern to create a specifically shaped light is not usually thought of as a special effect. It does not move, and in many ways it is used too often to be thought of as 'special'. But a device that slots into the same aperture and rotates the gobo as well as holding it is 'special'.

Not as subtle perhaps as other available devices – the rotation of a shape is by its very nature rather repetitive. It therefore does not produce the effect of rippling water or some such erratic movement. There are in fact no natural rotational movements that it can be used to re-create and very few day-to-day mechanical ones. It can, however, work well in combination with animation wheels. Also the double rotator, in which two independently moving gobos rotate at possibly different speeds

The Gobo rotator (DHA Ltd).

THE FASCINATION OF MOVEMENT

and directions, solves some of these problems. Experimentation is perhaps the best way to approach these.

Examples of use: Light through a rotating ceiling fan. Clock face. Cogs and other mechanical devices. Whirlpools. Laser effects.

Yo-Yo

A device to move a gobo in one direction or up and down only. Useful for repetitive effects and spot cues (that is, one-off moments).

Examples of use: waves, and other water effects. Sun rising or setting. Window or door being opened or shut.

Animation Wheels

These devices are the mainstay of many great stage moments. They consist of a wheel that rotates in front of a unit to produce a flickering quality in the light. The wheel is sufficiently outside the focal point of the unit such that its design does not project clearly, but instead interferes with the beam to cause a random or regular flicker effect in the light, the latter dependant on which wheel is in use.

The different wheels produce different effects. The most basic wheel – a disc with holes in – was originally known as a 'kk wheel'. Animation wheels are often used in combination with a gobo but may also be fitted to fresnel units.

Examples of use: (usually in combination with a gobo, *see* illustration below). Rippling water, waves. Reflected water. Flames. Clouds Rain. Snow. Light through trees. Passing train. Nightclub and disco effects.

Pattern 20: Coarse Radial Breakup
is particularly effective for animating light from a non-focusing source (non-profile lantern) whilst providing a minimal loss in intensity due to the high "white to black" ratio of the radial pattern. Also effective for similar uses to radial breakup

Pattern 21: Coarse Tangential Breakup
is most suitable for use in profile lanterns without the use of a gobo, in Fresnel or PC lanterns or on M16 mini parcans for flames etc.

Pattern 22: Colour Wheel
accepts five gels (held in place with standard paper fasteners) to give continual colour changes.

Examples of animation discs (DHA Ltd).

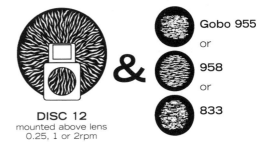

WATER

RIPPLING WATER

DISC 12
mounted above lens
0.25, 1 or 2rpm

Gobo 955
or
958
or
833

Use slower speeds for gentler or more distant movement. For rough water substitute a more 'wavy' gobo.

Examples of effects ideas (from DHA Ltd).

Flame Flicker

This is an old device design to fit the Pattern 123 – a Strand 500watt fresnel. Thus it can be used on any other similarly sized unit. It provides a soft flickery coloured light suggestive of the light from a reasonably lively burning fire.

Special Effect Units

Optical Devices

These are moving effect units that use an enclosed glass wheel rotating in front of a light source. Unlike animation effects (where the wheel is never clearly in focus) these attach to units specifically designed to allow a range of focus possibilities.

For example, they allow for the projection of a range of very precise images of clouds. Hence the catalogue range of Fleecy, Storm, Thunder, Cirrus, Nimbus and Cumulus. The units themselves are known as *Effects Projectors* or EPs (*see* illustration below).

NB: It is important to get the correct lens with these devices. This is dependent on the distance of throw and size of image required (if not, your snow effect can look like a hail of tennis balls!).

Examples of use: clouds. Running water. Flames. Rain. Snow. Nightclub, disco and other strange projected effects.

Lightning Effects

These are variously versions of high-power photographic flashes or single-shot strobe units. Naturally one could also use an ordinary profile with a lightning gobo. However, whilst this can be most effective, a gobo does not carry the authenticity, in brightness or speed, of a real lightning flash – the special lightning devices do.

Examples of use: lightning, entrance of Demon King.

Strobes

Units that flash a bright flood of light with a fast decay and the ability to reactivate almost instantaneously. They can be single or multi-flash – that is, one or many sources. Can come with variable speed and flash patterns. Local or remote control available.

Examples of use: lightning. Tube train. General disorientation. Slow motion effect. Disco.

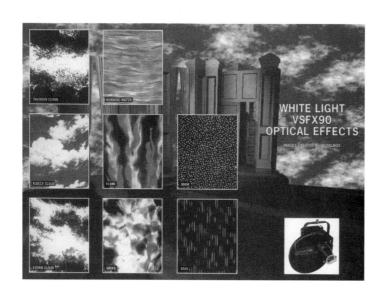

Special effects (White Light Ltd).

Arcline/Flexiflash

Small strobes enclosed in lengths of transparent plastic, Arcline being more rigid than Flexiflash.

Examples of use: lightning. Lightning bolts. Comet. Tube train. Disco.

Ropelight

Small bulbs enclosed in lengths of flexible transparent plastic

Examples of use: gives the appearance of movement as bulbs 'chase' along the lengths of the tube. Good for machinery. Computers. Around scenic pieces where appropriate. Musicals. Disco.

Festoon

String of bulbs on a single circuit. Like a ropelight but simpler – that is, no control on single bulbs – all or nothing. Usually any domestic bulb can be used – that is, standard b.c. fitting. Coloured bulbs can be used.

Examples of use: around scenic pieces where appropriate (Musicals), Disco or Party. More than one string can be interwoven to then act like a ropelight by alternating from one to another – three strings needed to give the appearance of movement along the length.

Scanners and Helicopters

Narrow beams of light projected from devices that spin and/or tumble.

Examples of use: hi-tech special effects – sci-fi. Futuristic machinery. Disco.

Fuzz Lights/Beacons

Flashing lights (beacons) that can revolve (fuzz lights), as on the top of emergency vehicles.

Examples of use: off-stage emergency events/vehicles. Hi-tech special effects – sci-fi. Futuristic machinery. Disco.

Tubular Ripple

A revolving tube with slots that turns in front of a flood-like light source to give the effect of distant flowing or rippling water.

Examples of use: good on backcloths to suggest distant waves on a horizon. Water effects over a large area – for example, swimming pool.

Star Cloths

A black cloth into which is woven a series of small lighting sources, or fibre optics to produce the effect of a field of stars.

Examples of use: stars. Nightclubs. Disco.

CONCLUSION

Movement in light – whether as a naturalistic effect or, more pertinently, as a cue, is a powerful tool to set mood and pace, and we should not forget it when we come to the planning of cues in later chapters.

For now it is worth noting that as part of a stage picture, moving light can be both visually attractive and dramatically instructive. It plays a strong role in defining location, atmosphere and in both supporting and creating mood.

Chapter Summary

- Movement fascinates the eye, no less with moving light.
- The speed allocated to changes of light dictates mood.
- Movement in light creates mood and/or focuses attention
- Fast cues are dramatic and aggressive.
- Slow cues are passive, gentle and moody.
- Some slow cues are so slow as to be imperceptible.
- In certain contexts even fast cues can go unnoticed.
- Split timings allow greater control of the movement of light.

6 EMOTIONAL COLOUR

Arguably the most potentially emotive and strangely personal component of theatre lighting is that of colour.

Colour is a subject about which most of us have strong opinions. Whether choosing a car or a carpet, socks or frocks, most of us have definite ideas on what colours we like and what colours we do not like – to the extent that we often say we 'hate' or 'love' them. To an audience colour can also become a strong communicator.

WHERE COLOUR COMES FROM

The first point that should be understood on this subject is that all the light we use on stage is coloured light.

A lantern (without any added colour medium) projects light of certain wavelengths that combine to create a very white colour, but a colour nonetheless. We may, incorrectly, call this 'white light', but if we compare the light from this lantern with that from another untainted 'white light' source – that is, a candle, a common light bulb, or another theatre unit of a different wattage – we soon see that the light from these, although not strikingly colourful, inhabits a range of 'whitenesses' – that is, they do not all produce the same colour of 'white light'. Even the same lantern when dimmed will appear a warmer white than when set at a brighter level. (This can be corrected – see Colour Correction, page 72).

The light from the sun that many would regard as the reference point for a natural 'white light' colour, also occupies a range of colour. This range depends on the atmospheric conditions that the light meets as it passes through our atmosphere. As we discovered in Chapter 2 this feature is called scattering. Scattering dictates that certain wavelengths within the light (that is, certain colours) are more or less dispersed depending on what they pass through. If more blue wavelengths are scattered, the light appears redder. If more red wavelengths are scattered, the light appears bluer or whiter.

SEEING COLOUR

A light source that is white in appearance contains a mixture of all the visible spectrum – a fairly even mixture of all the possible wavelengths of light that our eyes can distinguish. It is only when a part of this spectrum is isolated that we see what we identify as colour.

Although a colour often has, by its very nature, a dominance of certain wavelengths of light, it can also still have a lesser amount of all the other wavelengths – it is then said to contain some 'white' light. A colour that has no white light content is referred to as a saturated colour (see also page 68).

There is no colour without light, and at very low levels of light our eyes cannot read colour. Interestingly, at such low levels we are still able to discern both shape and movement – probably because these would have been of more self-preserving use to our distant animal ancestors than the ability to discern colour.

Even if the light level is increased, and the eye becomes able to recognize some colour

The human eye.

The retina is a layer of neurons that are sensitive to light. There are two types: rods and cones. Rods are sensitive to low levels of light, whilst cones work well in bright light and distinguish well between different wavelengths – i.e. they see colour.

   The fovea is a small area which has only a great concentration of cones, and thus gives the greatest degree of detail and colour.

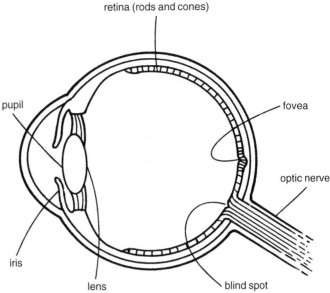

BELOW:
The creation of colour.

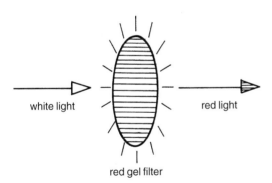

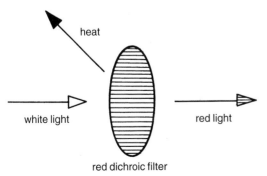

differences, they remain muted. (Think of seeing cars parked on a street on a dark evening.)

   Eventually the eye has enough light available to see colour clearly. For example, a blue object when hit with 'white light' absorbs all wavelengths of light except a certain specific range, which it reflects, and we see as blue.

   The wide variety of colours we see around us are simply different mixtures of wavelengths being reflected into our eyes, analysed by the brain and interpreted as colour.

USING COLOUR ON STAGE

Colours are produced in theatre lanterns in a fashion similar to the normal reflection of light, either by using a medium to absorb certain wavelengths (a filter) or by refracting them (using a dichroic glass – *see* illustration left).

   Because an object only reflects certain wavelengths of light, we need those wavelengths to be present in the light illuminating it, in order for them to be reflected back to us. Thus, for

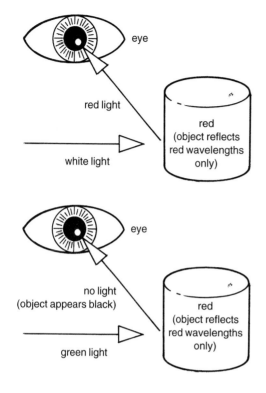

The perception of colour.

example, a red object seen under green light appears black (*see* illustration above). On occasion, strange things can happen when using strong colours – that is, a limited range of wavelengths. An object of an apparent colour can unexpectedly reflect something completely different, because the light hitting it only contains a few wavelengths that the object can reflect.

Thus, strongly coloured light can radically change the appearance of an object. This is something a lighting designer can make good use of on stage, particularly when lighting the set or costumes.

Obviously, the same is true for paler colours. They also alter the appearance of the things they are lighting, but to a lesser degree. This is particularly relevant to the work of a lighting

designer, as it is the paler colours that are used more frequently to illuminate the stage.

As with soft versus hard-edged beams (*see* page 51), and slow versus fast movement in light (*see* page 60) once again this area can be divided into the passive (pale colours) and the aggressive or dominant (strong/dark colours).

It is precisely because the paler colours are passive and persuade more gently that they are more commonly used on stage. Their influence is less dramatic and more subtle. With paler colours, there is the opportunity to persuade the audience emotionally without their being too aware of how it is happening.

Where one draws the line between passive and aggressive in describing or using colour on stage is, of course, very dependent on context and personal taste.

Aggressive colours, often saturated colours that are dark or rich, make powerful statements. The colour wheels in the illustrations demonstrate some of the ideas that such strong colours can generate when we use them on stage.

Whilst strong, aggressive colours serve on stage to make very 'loud' dramatic statements, they do tend to swamp or overwhelm. This is particularly the case when they are used to light performers. It is simply the case that for most of the time we do not want to see actors bathed in dark red, blue, green or yellow light! For this reason, the darker colours are used on stage more rarely. Paler, passive colours are more commonly used, because they echo the natural light of the real world that is also rarely strongly coloured.

Pale ambers, straws, delicate pinks and airy blues all project well onto human skin tones – they echo the colour range of real light. On stage, however, we can allow ourselves a wider range of these 'true to life' colours than would strictly adhere to reality. In this way we can explore a greater range of moods, and sometimes slightly exaggerate them for dramatic effect (*see* Chapter 7).

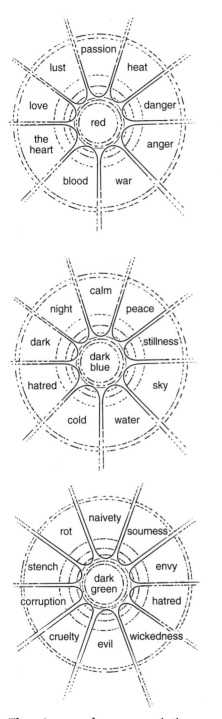

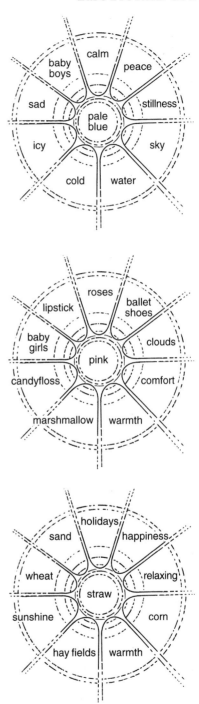

The primary colours – associations.

Hues and tints – associations.

Light Relief

A common use of colour on stage is the costuming of the stage crew in black. Scene changes are often lit with a dark blue wash of light – a substitute for darkness but one in which the crew can see what they are doing.

To do this a dark blue filter is used, and some of the available filters contain a surprising amount of red that is normally not visible.

Until on come the stage crew in their blacks – or as it unexpectedly now appears their blacks, purples, dark reds, maroons, mauves, and so on.

Colours, especially as replicators of sunlight and other real sources, break down into having the appearance of warmth or coolness. A colour either adds warmth to a scene or cools it down. However subtle this colour may be, this distinction remains true. Although perhaps the very 'thinnest' of colours may be considered as being more neutral in effect than anything else.

The distinction between warm and cool colours is also true when one colour is seen against another – unless two light beams are of the same colour, one will appear to be cooler or warmer than the other. Of course, the same colour can appear warm or cool depending on what it is compared with.

As a generalization, warm colours are used for comedies, romances and musicals, whilst cold colours are preferred for tragedies, mysteries and thrillers.

In Practice

As the illustration below shows, manufacturers provide colour in sheets or rolls. Each colour is identified by number, and there may be as many

The manufacture of colour (Lee Filters).

as 400 colours in a manufacturer's range. In what has become a very competitive market, new colours are being added all the time. One of Lee Filters' latest additions is number 778 – Millennium Gold, added in the year 2000.

A colour is cut to fit the colour frame or holder that is pertinent to the lantern being used. For identification purposes the colour number is usually written onto the 'gel' using a wax pencil.

The colour frame holds the thin material in place even when subjected to the inevitable heat that is a by-product of the light source.

Even with such a wide choice, the lighting designer may still feel that the colour he or she has in mind is not present in the range, in which case, by placing two colours on top of each other, a new colour may be created. This is known as 'subtractive colour mixing'.

It is called 'subtractive' because each different colour takes away further from the total spectrum being projected from the lantern. If more and more colours are added, or very dark colours used, the end result will be very dim, until finally no light will be escaping!

Colour (gel) held in the lantern.

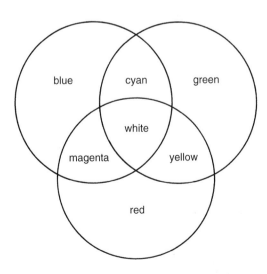

Primary colour mixing in light.

A more common kind of colour mixing is created when different colours are projected towards the stage in different lanterns. From our understanding of colour (*see* pages 67–8) we should realize that in this case the resultant mix is 'additive colour mixing' – 'additive' because each colour adds to the spectral range in view. If all colours were added together in this way we would see the whole spectrum – that is, 'white light'.

Although not of any really specific use to the lighting designer, it is nevertheless worth noting that in light the three primary colours are green, red and blue (*see* illustration left).

It is obviously the case that nearly all productions incorporate additive mixing. Only if one colour is being used in all units will this not be so.

As no two lanterns can actually occupy the same physical space, additive colour mixing produces both a colour mix and shadow infill (*see* illustration overleaf).

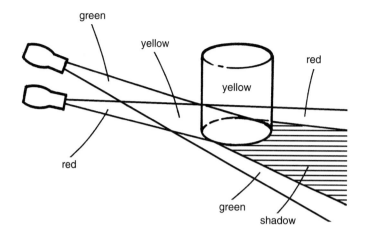

Additive colour mixing.

The infilling of projected shadows with colour can be knowingly used by a lighting designer to good effect. It is an effective way in which strong colour can be used in a scene. It simultaneously avoids colouring the actors with too much inappropriate (unreal) colour but nevertheless is subtly readable by the audience. A strong colour directed from above or behind the performer also works particularly well in this respect.

Strong colours like the primaries are not as often used as the lighter hues as we have discussed. Only with the use of such heavy colour is the audience itself going to be aware of additive colour mixing. In practice, the lighting designer develops a sensitivity to what lighter colours blend well with each other in this way.

The one place where shadow infill does not apply is when light is being projected onto a flat surface – where the surface itself does not produce shadow. Thus it is on the back wall of a set – the cyclorama – that additive colour mixing works particularly effectively and in its purest form.

In the illustration overleaf, rows of cyc' units and battens represent the usual way of lighting a cyclorama. Battens are flood units ganged together – typically three or four units in each batten.

SPECIALIZED COLOUR FILTERS

Certain colours are manufactured that perform specific specialized roles, although some of them can also be thought of as colours in their own right and used as such, along with the other more 'normal' colours.

Colour Correction

In discussing 'normal' light sources, we noted that different light sources appear to radiate different shades of 'white light'. Daylight is a different colour compared with a theatre unit using a tungsten/halogen bulb. Fluorescent lighting units also broadcast a different range of wavelengths of light, and so on.

To counter this fact, filters are produced that convert one source to another and they do this by literally filtering out the unwanted wavelengths.

For example, another source that produces a different colour 'white light' is the light that emanates from units that rely on discharge bulbs rather than the more usual tungsten/halogen (*see* page 31). In this case, colour correction filters are often used to realign the colour output of the discharging units (often follow-spots) to that of the rest of the lighting rig.

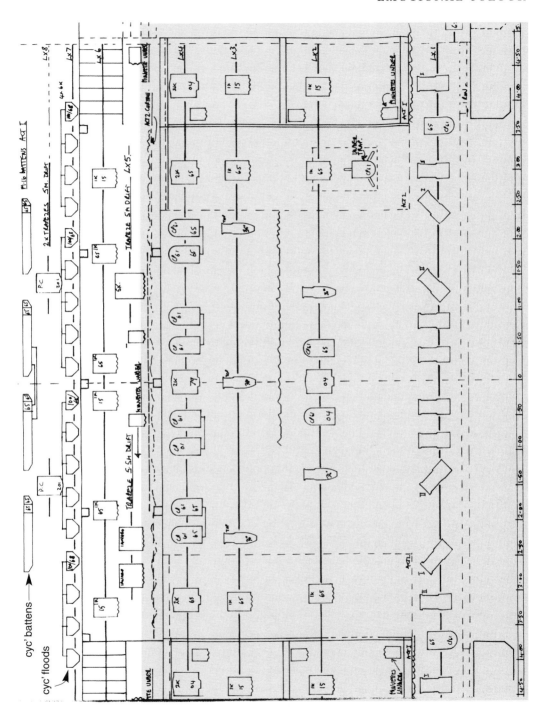

Cyclorama lighting – part of a typical design.

These are especially important filters in the fields of drama that are recorded by an instrument other than the human eye, that is, on film. The human eye/brain is capable of making allowances for these colour discrepancies, it 'understands' them, whereas on film the lighting simply develops a pink, green or some such tint in an inappropriate manner.

In theatre terms, colour correction is used in a number of ways:

* As a colour in its own right.
* To convert one source to another. As in the example of the discharge units above.
* Specifically to convert a tungsten/halogen source to a wavelength similar to daylight – that is, to use the real colour of daylight.

Neutral Density

Another filter is used (again mostly in photography or film) to reduce the light output from a unit without dimming it. This is useful in two ways:

* To correct a unit that, although paired with another on the same dimmer, appears to be producing more light.
* To reduce the light output without dimming and thus avoiding a colour shift – remembering that as a unit is dimmed it becomes warmer in colour.

The following tables (*see* pages 74–6) are taken from the colour correction filters listing produced by Lee Filters, one of the biggest producers in this field. In their catalogue they

Colour Conversion Filters (Lee Filters)							
Product	Description	Kelvin	Mired Shift	Transmission Y%	Absorption	Chromaticity Coordinates x	y
Tungsten Light Conversion							
200 Double C.T.B.	Converts Tungsten to Daylight	3200K to 26,000K (approx.)	−274	16.2	0.79	0.179	0.155
201 Full C.T.B.	Converts Tungsten to Photographic Daylight	3200K to 5700K	−137	34.0	0.47	0.228	0.233
281 Three-quarters C.T.B.	Converts Tungsten to Daylight	3200K to 5000K	−112	45.5	0.35	0.239	0.258
202 Half C.T.B.	Converts Tungsten to Daylight	3200K to 4300K	−78	54.9	0.26	0.261	0.273
203 Quarter C.T.B.	Converts Tungsten to Daylight	3200K to 3600K	−35	69.2	0.16	0.285	0.294
218 Eighth C.T.B.	Converts Tungsten to Daylight	3200K 3400K	−18	81.3	0.09	0.299	0.307
Daylight Conversion							
204 Full C.T.O.	Converts Daylight to Tungsten Light	6500K to 3200K	+159	55.4	0.26	0.437	0.392
285 Three-quarters C.T.O.	Converts Daylight to Tungsten Light	6500K to 3600K	+124	61.3	0.21	0.400	0.387
205 Half C.T.O.	Converts Daylight to Tungsten Light	6500K to 3800K	+109	70.8	0.15	0.374	0.364

Colour Conversion Filters (Lee Filters) *continued*

Product	Description	Kelvin	Mired Shift	Transmission Y%	Absorption	Chromaticity Coordinates x	y
206 Quarter C.T.O.	Converts Daylight to Tungsten Light	6500K to 4600K	+64	79.1	0.10	0.346	0.346
223 Eighth C.T.O.	Converts Daylight to Tungsten Light	6500K to 5550K	+26	85.2	0.07	0.328	0.332
207 Full C.T.O. + .3ND	Converts Daylight to Tungsten and reduces light 1 Stop	6500K to 3200K	+159	32.5	0.49	0.435	0.386
208 Full C.T.O. + .6ND	Converts Daylight to Tungsten and reduces light 2 Stops	6500K to 3200K	+159	15.6	0.81	0.442	0.394
441 Full C.T. Straw	Converts Daylight to Tungsten Light with yellow bias	6500K to 3200K	+160	57.3	0.24	0.426	0.407
442 Half C.T. Straw	Converts Daylight to Tungsten Light with yellow bias	6500K to 4300K	+81	71.2	0.15	0.370	0.378
443 Quarter C.T. Straw	Converts Daylight to Tungsten Light with yellow bias	6500K to 5100K	+42	79.8	0.10	0.338	0.349
444 Eighth C.T. Straw	Converts Daylight to Tungsten Light with yellow bias	6500K to 5700K	+20	83.1	0.08	0.323	0.332

Neutral Density

Product	Description	Transmission Y%	Absorption	Chromaticity Coordinates x	y
298 .15ND	Reduces light ½ Stop, without changing colour	69.3	0.16	0.311	0.319
209 .3ND	Reduces light 1 Stop, without changing colour	51.2	0.29	0.310	0.319
210 .6ND	Reduces light 2 Stops, without changing colour	23.5	0.63	0.308	0.317
211 .9ND	Reduces light 3 Stops, without changing colour	13.7	0.86	0.310	0.322
299 1.2ND	Reduces light 4 Stops, without changing colour	6.6	1.18	0.308	0.315

Colour Correction Filters (Lee Filters)

Product	Description	Transmission Y%	Absorption	Chromaticity Coordinates x	y
Arc Correction (Carbon-Regular)					
212 LC.T. Yellow (Y1)	Reduces Colour Temperature of low carbon arcs to 3200K	88.7	0.05	0.340	0.363
213 White Flame Green	Corrects White Flame Carbon arcs by absorbing ultra-violet	80.0	0.10	0.317	0.359

(continued overleaf)

Colour Correction Filters (Lee Filters) *continued*

Product		Description	Transmission Y%	Absorption	Chromaticity Coordinates x	y
Arc Correction (Carbon-Colour Balanced)						
230	Super Correction LC.T. Yellow	Converts Yellow carbon arc (of low colour temperature) to Tungsten	41.9	0.38	0.367	0.368
232	Super Correction W.F. Green to Tungsten	Converts White Flame arc to 3200K, for use with Tungsten film	37.4	0.43	0.423	0.385
Arc Correction (Compact Source)						
236	HMI (to Tungsten)	Converts HMI to 3200K, for use with Tungsten film	58.2	0.24	0.426	0.376
237	CID (to Tungsten)	Converts CID to 3200K, for use with Tungsten film	38.5	0.41	0.430	0.365
238	CSI (to Tungsten)	Converts CSI to 3200K, for use with Tungsten film	29.8	0.53	0.372	0.331
Fluorescent Correction System						
241	Lee Fluorescent 5700 Kelvin	Converts Tungsten to Fluorescent light of 5700K (cool white/daylight)	27.4	0.56	0.231	0.290
242	Lee fluorescent 4300 Kelvin	Converts Tungsten to Fluorescent light of 4300K (white)	37.3	0.43	0.262	0.346
243	Lee Fluorescent 3600 Kelvin	Converts Tungsten to Fluorescent light of 3600K (warm white)	45.7	0.34	0.286	0.370
219	Lee Fluorescent Green	General Tungsten to Fluorescent correction for use when colour temperature is unknown	31.0	0.51	0.219	0.334

The above correction filters are to be used in conjunction with an appropriate Lee FL-B Fluorescent to Tungsten or Lee FL-D Fluorescent to Daylight camera filter.

Plus Green – *Used on Daylight and Tungsten light sources to provide green cast when used in conjunction with discharge lighting.*

244	Lee Plus Green	Approximately equivalent to CC30 Green camera filter	74.2	0.12	0.324	0.388
245	Half Plus Green	Approximately equivalent to CC15 Green camera filter	81.7	0.08	0.319	0.355
246	Quarter Plus Green	Approximately equivalent to CC075 Green camera filter	84.6	0.07	0.315	0.337
278	Eighth Plus Green	Provides very slight green cast	87.7	0.06	0.313	0.327

The above correction filters are to be used in conjunction with an appropriate Lee FL-B Fluorescent to Tungsten or Lee FL-D Fluorescent to Daylight camera filter.

Colour Correction Filters (Lee Filters) *continued*					
Product	Description	Transmission Y%	Absorption	Chromaticity Coordinates x	y

Minus Green – Used on lighting to eliminate unwanted green cast created by discharge light sources on film.

Product	Description	Transmission Y%	Absorption	x	y
247 Lee Minus Green	Approximately equivalent to CC30 Magenta camera filter	57.8	0.22	0.325	0.279
248 Half Minus Green	Approximately equivalent to CC15 Magenta camera filter	72.0	0.14	0.317	0.297
249 Quarter Minus Green	Approximately equivalent to CC075 Magenta camera filter	82.4	0.08	0.312	0.307
279 Eighth Minus Green	Provides very slight correction	86.5	0.06	0.312	0.311
Ultra-Violet Absorption					
226 Lee UV	Transmission of less than 50% at 410nm	91.5	0.04	0.314	0.321

put them under two headings, 'Colour Correction' and 'Colour Conversion'.

Diffusion

Finally, there are filters that diffuse the light output of a lantern. They are often also called 'frosts' and they are made in varying degrees – so that the diffusion can be of varying strengths. Sometimes they are combined with a colour – for example, 'Blue Frost', although the lighting designer can always combine a diffusion gel with any colour from the range.

There also exist *directional diffusions*, also known as 'silks'. These are polarized filters that diffuse the light in one direction only depending on how they are put before the unit. They are particularly useful when the lighting designer is trying with too few lights to light an object or area in one direction only – for example, a tall or wide cyclorama, or a narrow walkway on stage.

The table (*see* page 78) shows Lee Filters' range of these products.

Colour Changers

As we have seen when discussing colour, the choice that a lighting designer makes in this area greatly affects the emotional or dramatic message being sold to the audience. The ability to change the colour of the light coming from a source allows for a greater range of such moments in the journey through a play.

Various devices are manufactured to allow for this to be the case:

Colour Wheel
A remote-control device that rotates in front of a lantern, presenting a number of colours before the beam. Usually divided into five sections. Only one colour can be in use at any one time.

Colour Semaphore
A remote-control device that allows for a number of colours to be flagged in front of a lantern – usually four options. No colour, a single colour or any mix of the four colours can be used.

Scroller
A remote-control device that allows a roll of joined colours to 'scroll' across the front of the lantern. The colour options vary by manufacturer but are typically between sixteen and thirty-two different colours per scroll. The scroller can also stop with a half-and-half mix. The speed of change can be dictated and thus a

Diffusion (Lee Filters)				
Product	**Description**	**Transmission %**	**Stop Value**	**Special Note**
216 White Diffusion		36	1½	Rolls also available in 1.52m (60in) width
416 Three Quarter White Diffusion		50	1	
250 Half White Diffusion	Used for soft light effects. Manufactured on a tough polyester base in a range of seven strengths	60	¾	
450 Three Eighth White Diffusion		63	⅔	
251 Quarter White Diffusion		80	⅓	
252 Eighth White Diffusion		>85	<¼	
452 Sixteenth White Diffusion		>85	<¼	
400 LeeLux	A dense white diffuser used for soft light effects (125 micron polyester base)	36	1½	
217 Blue Diffusion	As White Diffusion but with the addition of eighth CTB	36	1½	⅛ C.T. Blue
228 Brushed Silk	Directional soft light effect used for scattering light in one direction only	60	¾	
224 Daylight Blue Frost	Frosts are used for soft light effects and can include tungsten correction or neutral density	22	2½	Full C.T. Blue
225 Neutral Density Frost		25	2	.6 Neutral Density
255 Hollywood Frost		83	<⅓	
253 Hampshire Frost	Light frost effect	>85	<¼	
256 Half Hampshire Frost	Extra Light frost effect	>85	<¼	
257 Quarter Hampshire Frost	Extra Light frost effect	>85	<¼	
258 Eighth Hampshire Frost	Extra Light frost effect	>85	<¼	
410 Opal Frost	Used for softening spotlight beam edges without altering shape	71	½	
420 Light Opal Frost	Similar characteristics to Opal Frost but less diffuse	>85	<¼	

continuous colour change of some subtlety created as an effect in its own right.

Changing colours in scrollers is a lengthy and expensive business. Each colour has to be a precise length, and attached precisely to its neighbour. Such scrolls are often made up to suit a general use, as shown in the boxed example (*opposite page*).

Colours Chosen to Place in Scrollers

1. From the 'White Light Ltd' hire stock, a mixture of vivid and more subtle hues to suit any customer.

Frame 0	Rosco	54	Special Lavender	Frame 8	Rosco	00	Clear
Frame 1	Rosco	25	Orange Red	Frame 9	Lee	202	½ CT Blue
Frame 2	Rosco	312	Canary Yellow	Frame 10	Lee	201	Full CT Blue
Frame 3	Rosco	339	Broadway Pink	Frame 11	Lee	200	Double CT Blue
Frame 4	Rosco	21	Golden Amber	Frame 12	Rosco	68	Sky Blue
Frame 5	Lee	204	Full CT Orange	Frame 13	Rosco	385	Royal Blue
Frame 6	Rosco	03	Dark Bastard Amber	Frame 14	Lee	120	Dark Blue
Frame 7	Rosco	13	Straw Tint	Frame 15	Rosco	349	Fisher Fuchsia

2. From Rada's own equipment and thus to suit a range of mostly 'straight' dramatic plays.

Frame 0	Lee	053	Paler Lavender	Frame 16	Lee	156	Chocolate
Frame 1	Lee	058	Lavender	Frame 17	Lee	152	Pale Gold
Frame 2	Lee	170	Deep Lavender	Frame 18	Lee	776	Nectarine
Frame 3	Lee	716	Mikkel Blue	Frame 19	Lee	777	Rust
Frame 4	Lee	197	Alice Blue	Frame 20	Lee	213	White Flame Green
Frame 5	Lee	711	Cold Blue	Frame 21	Lee	138	Pale Green
Frame 6	Lee	719	Colour Wash Blue	Frame 22	Lee	139	Primary Green
Frame 7	Lee	200	Double CT Blue	Frame 23	Lee	116	Medium Blue Green
Frame 8	Lee	201	Full CT Blue	Frame 24	Lee	735	Velvet Green
Frame 9	Lee	218	⅛ CT Blue	Frame 25	Lee	104	Deep Amber
Frame 10	Lee	130	Clear	Frame 26	Lee	022	Dark Amber
Frame 11	Lee	443	¼ CT Straw	Frame 27	Lee	026	Bright Red
Frame 12	Lee	764	Sun Colour Straw	Frame 28	Lee	128	Bright Pink
Frame 13	Lee	009	Pale Amber Gold	Frame 29	Lee	126	Mauve
Frame 14	Lee	204	Full CT Orange	Frame 30	Lee	363	Special Medium Blue
Frame 15	Lee	230	Super Correction LCT Yellow	Frame 31	Lee	071	Tokyo Blue

See also scrollers in use as part of the design example on page 145.

NB: It has to be noted that so-called 'intelligent luminaires' allow for colour changing as one of their basic functions. These devices incorporate prismatic colour creation, or colour changing by use of colour wheel or semaphore or a mixture of all of these.

Light Relief

The design arena can be very frustrating, and colour use is no less a minefield than anything else. I once backlit a wicked witch with a blood red gel, thinking it gave her a particularly ferocious look, only to be asked later by a friend, 'Was there an electric bar fire behind that actor in the last act – she looked in danger of catching fire!'

Taking time to make sure that the assumptions you are making are going to be shared by the audience is worth the effort. On the other hand, there is always one!

Colour scrollers – without scrolls of colour – showing the tubing and gearing.

Conclusion

Colour is a strong tool, best used with great subtlety.

Subtle colour use can coax, insinuate and influence us into a mood or feeling without our noticing it. And yet also nothing perhaps works so effectively as using a narrow range of colour in a production (perhaps no filters at all) only to burst suddenly into strong colour for a particular dramatic climax.

The use of an analogous colour scheme – a range of colours that contains a common dominant hue – is highly effective in projecting mood. It is especially effective in helping to define a locale or general ambience across the length and breadth of a whole production.

On stage, the lighting designer has enormous power to influence the appearance of the drama, and colour is one of the strongest tools in their repertoire. In using colour they even act in a god-like manner to dictate the colour of the sun itself.

Chapter Summary

- All light is coloured light.
- In theatre terms, there is no definable thing as 'white light'.
- Higher levels of light are needed to see colour than either shape or movement.
- Strongly coloured light can radically change the appearance of an object.
- Pale colours are passive, strong colours are aggressive.
- Generally, dominant dark colours are less frequently used.
- Pale colours are nearly always used on stage somewhere.
- Colour is either warm or cold.
- The warmth or coldness of a colour is dependent on what it is being compared to.
- A narrow colour scheme may help define location and/or mood.
- Warm colours for comedy, cold colours for tragedy.

7   THE CREATION OF MOOD

The concept of atmosphere or mood has been touched upon many times in the chapters leading up to this one. The creation of a theatrical mood is integral to everything we do when we manipulate light on stage.

This remains true whether we are using light to illuminate, to show form, to add colour or create movement. All these aspects are in themselves inherently mood creating, and the degree of skill employed to manipulate them will finally determine the effectiveness of the mood seen on stage, and possibly of the drama itself.

In the preceding chapters we have concentrated our thinking on how one or more lanterns affect the appearance of a single object. This can be summarized as decisions concerning the following considerations:

* Intensity – how much light do we need?
* Position – shallow or oblique, normal or strange angles?
* Shape – to depict objects, add texture, or control spill.
* Colour – to make strong statements, and/or set tone.
* Appearance – how may the appearance of movement in light add to the stage effect we are trying to create?
* Control – how best to manipulate the lighting? The speed of cues and so on.

A lighting designer has to develop an understanding of all these facets in order to be able to put together a framework within which to work.

Through practice and experience, a visual vocabulary of ideas is built up about how to use

Mood in lighting – Sleeping Beauty *(Polka Theatre).*

light effectively. This knowledge will, in turn, develop into a personal style, and be drawn on for each new production, the lighting designer applying it in different ways on each occasion. Each of these occasions will by necessity, however, deal with the creation of mood.

What Do We Mean by Mood?

Mood can be tragic or comic, can be strong and dominating or subtle and suggestive. It can be used to imply a real location or an internalized truth. For example, the blistering heat of a hot summer's day in a hayfield, or an intense feeling of persecution and oppression. It can be as simple as a single light striking the face of an actor or complex enough to need to be expressed by a rig of four hundred lanterns.

A mood can be subtle or crashingly obvious. A mood can be sustained for a second, or a whole performance. A mood can change in an instant, or slowly over the course of three hours or more. A mood can unsettle or relax, provoke or lull, anaesthetize or cajole. A mood can make you think, keep you fooled, take you away from yourself or bring you down to earth with a bump.

In many ways, mood *is* theatre, and the possibilities are inexhaustible.

Creating Mood

The first two challenges involved with the creation of mood are identifying the mood required and then manipulating light to create it. The sources section at the end of this chapter is a guide to some of the ways in which a lighting designer may seek help in the former of these, and the rest of the book seeks to aid in the latter. But even when these two hurdles are cleared, there remains the problem of sustaining the mood.

Generally speaking, it is always going to be helpful when working on a production for the lighting designer to have strong ideas about the piece, and be enthusiastically committed to them. However a lighting designer can spend a lot of time and energy developing such ideas only to find that the other members of the design team may be in disagreement. If not addressed, this issue can lead to the great tension between director, designer and lighting designer. It requires careful consideration.

The key to solving this potential problem is communication. Certainly there is no point in getting carried away with ideas about the overall mood of a piece unless you are fairly sure the other team members are with you. Having to abandon the mood that you have carefully crafted can be a painful business.

In a plotting session (*see* page 133) you will often have to state your beliefs clearly in order to defend what your lighting rig is doing – so be prepared to do so, and also remain flexible within the context of the mood you are creating – there are nearly always alternative ways to the same result. In any case, make sure that your preparation includes, rather than excludes, as many people as possible.

Mood and the Creation of a Lighting Design

As mood is integral to nearly all aspects of lighting a production, and as the preceding chapters have covered the essential aspects of a lighting design, this seems a good place to look comprehensively at the whole process of creating a lighting design.

To create the lighting for any single production, a lighting designer has to address a number of objectives. These are derived from the text itself, from conversations with the director or designer, from seeing a rehearsal of the piece, or from the lighting designer's own imagination.

The actual process of lighting a production and of plotting cues is discussed further in Chapter 12.

What the lighting designer has to achieve on any piece will vary from production to production. But in general terms it can easily be derived by referring to our definition of what lighting is capable of in Chapter 2.

The lighting designer will need to assess which of the following categories applies; when, in what manner, and to what degree. Heavily involved in these decisions will be the overriding consideration of what mood, or moods, the lighting designer needs to create within the piece.

* *Illuminate* – what type of equipment will be required to show the audience what it needs to see?
* *Separate* – do parts of the stage area need to be isolated or defined?
* *Embellish* – does anything on stage need 'dressing'? – i.e. so it looks appropriate to the scene.
* *Locate* – does the lighting need to define the moment? The season, the weather, the time, or the locality – either on all the stage or a part of it.
* *Punctuate* – are special moments required to punctuate the drama? That is, by the way cues are plotted and operated.
* *Pinpoint* – is equipment needed to highlight or further define or identify important areas on stage for purely dramatic purpose?
* *Disguise* – is it necessary to make sure that at certain moments particular areas on stage are not lit? The spill from lights and the shadow they create is relevant here.
* *Create Mood* – how are the above to be achieved (regarding use of angle, colour, shape, and so on), in order that the appropriate dramatic mood is obtained? Is any extra equipment required for this?
* *Change Mood* – is any extra equipment required to allow for the *change* of dramatic mood throughout the piece?
* *Create Spectacle* – do any particular moments, or the piece as a whole, require special effects or highlighting that could be described as creating visual impact?

As we noted earlier, many of the above categories overlap or interrelate with each other. No serious lighting designer would actually list them as I have done – instinct and experience work together so that a list such as this would be far too clumsy a method of approach. However to work efficiently, a lighting designer does need a methodical approach of some kind.

IN PRACTICE

A good method of creating a lighting design is for the lighting designer to put together a list of what the production requires from the lighting alongside a list of equipment and an understanding of the venue (*see* example in illustration overleaf).

The method outlined may be too rigid for some. A more organic approach may be preferred. In which case, there can be said to be two variations in the general way in which lighting for a production can be designed.

Either: lighting is designed to achieve every specific that is understood to be required for a production.

Or: lighting is designed to offer a range of possibilities to the creative team (director, designer, lighting designer), rather than specifics. In the plotting session, the lighting designer is offering options from a palette of visual possibilities, not initially knowing how any element may be used, or when.

Both these techniques have their advantages, and neither of them stands alone. For instance, whilst it may be that a design attempts to cover all requirements, sometimes the logistics of a production will be prohibitive (for example, there may not be enough equipment available, or an insufficient number of dimmers, or too simplistic a lighting control). In this case, the lighting designer will have to concentrate on a smaller prioritized list of objectives than they would like, and hope to cover other areas

BIRDS ON THE WING - Needs List	
GENERAL COVERS:	Band
Interior Club Night	Dance numbers
Interior Club - Working Light / Day	Aisles
Exterior Day - Sunny	
Exterior Night	EFFECTS:
Board Room	Mirror Ball(s)
	Follow Spot
SET DRESSING:	Lightning
Wall (exterior)	
Door (s)	PRACTICALS:
Portraits	Lamp Post
Small stage	Acropolis Sign
	Stars
SPECIALS:	
Lamp post	NB: Follow Spots required.

The needs list.

with an element of improvisation at the plotting session – hoping the design offers a palette of alternatives other than those originally identified.

On the other hand, whilst it may feel more creative to invent the lighting from a 'visual palette' at the plotting session, the palette itself must have been put together with a range of useable lighting that itself must be derived from an understanding of what the production requires.

Perhaps the two methods are closer than they appear, the real difference between them being more one of presentation and method than anything else.

SOURCES

The inspiration required to make the necessary decisions about how the play, or moments in a play, are to look – the mood they are to have – can seem illusive. Indeed the concept of mood can be a difficult one to define, let alone create.

However, a lighting designer is not alone in having to find the appropriate mood for a piece, or without aids. The text and the play in rehearsal are there to prompt ideas, as are the other members of the creative team.

Directors and designers often communicate with lighting designers by example. Influences outside the production process are often sought, and those can be used as templates for the creation of mood. They fall into a number of categories.

Life

The most obvious reference, and one we have already been talking about, is that of real life. Your own photographs, or those from magazines or books of any type that show strong 'real life' images, can make useful references.

Not unlike photographs, paintings can also be of use.

Art

Reference to a painting or the work of a painter is common – indeed a whole production can be designed around such a visual reference.

The paintings of Rembrandt and other Dutch masters are commonly described as they make important use of chiaroscuro. The work of Caravaggio is also commonly referred to.

The work of the French Impressionists has a strong appeal, as does the expressionistic work of various artists, particularly from Germany. For example, the cartoons of George Grosz are often used for reference or to depict the decadency of pre-war Germany, and the work of Hogarth to depict the same in eighteenth-century England.

A famous example of using such a reference was Peter Brook's production of *Love's Labours Lost* for the RSC (1950) that took the paintings of Watteau as its theme and scenic template.

Media

References are often made to styles from other media – side-lighting may be imported from the world of dance, for example.

Inspiration can also be taken from the music to be used in a production itself.

More particularly, film style or even specific films can be required study. Film noir, with its shadowy low-key lighting, is a particular favourite. In fact, nearly any film with a strong sense of the visual could be usefully referred to, especially as in the age of the video they are usually accessible. Examples include Robert Weine's *The Cabinet of Dr Caligari*, Eisenstein's *Battleship Potemkin*, Kurosawa's *Ran*, Welles's *Citizen Kane*, Ridley Scott's *Blade Runner*, the work of Spielberg or Lucas, Bertolucci or Tim Burton – the list is seemingly endless.

Literature

As well as sources in the play itself, other descriptions from literature can be used to evoke images and promote ideas. For example, this passage from John Fletcher's poem 'Love's Emblems':

Now the lust spring is seen;
    Golden yellow, gaudy blue,
    Daintily invite the view:
Everywhere on every green
Roses blushing as they blow
    And enticing men to pull,
Lilies whiter than the snow,
    Woodbines of sweet honey full:
All love's emblems, and all cry,
'Ladies, if not plucked, we die.'

Or Milton's lines from 'Evening in Paradise':

Now came still evening on, and twilight grey
Had in her sober livery all things clad;

Other Work

The work of other lighting designers, seen by a member of the creative team, can also be used to suggest ideas for a new production. One should never be too proud to borrow or lend ideas – indeed this could be thought of as the highest form of flattery.

Sources of light from real life.

ABOVE: *A period illustration of London is used as reference and backdrop to this studio production of* The Art of Success – *designer Alison Cartlidge.*

Student lighting designers Sebastian Barraclough and David Bishop produce an inspiring piece of lighting for a project – Fanfare.

Lighting helping to create mood – The Lion, the Witch and the Wardrobe (*Contact Theatre*).

CONCLUSION

The creation of mood need not be the nightmare that it can at first appear to be. With a good understanding of the way light works and experience in manipulating it, mood can fall into place almost without trying.

However, in order to keep coming up with fresh ideas, a lighting designer needs to be open to as many influences and suggestions as possible. Otherwise the danger is that they will develop a style which, however appealing, may remain static, be considered out of date, and no longer required.

There is little more satisfying than realizing that you, as part of the creative team, have got the mood right for a production – and nothing is as clear as when you have 'got it right'.

Chapter Summary

- The creation of mood is central to all lighting design.
- Any light on stage is described with reference to its intensity, angle, shape, colour, movement, and how it is introduced to the audience.
- The manipulation of these factors creates mood.
- A lighting design is a mixture of the specific and the general.
- Anything can be usefully employed as both a source of, or means to communicate, ideas about mood.
- Mood can be thought of as just another word for style.
- Mood is integral to the theatre experience.
- The mood of a play can never be defined by the lighting alone.

8 MODERN LIGHTING THEORY

INTRODUCTION

The preceding chapters have dealt with the major aspects of theatre lighting – light, intensity, shape, colour, mood and even how to approach a complete design.

Although practitioners of stage lighting tend to learn and develop ideas and practices by doing, we have also found throughout history many notable commentators who have written down their discoveries.

By the late 1920s, and certainly into the 1930s, the use of electric lighting sources had revolutionized theatrical lighting sufficiently, and been around long enough, to warrant the appearance of the first 'how to' manuals, a good number of which were aimed at the amateur. These textbooks give us a comprehensive insight into the minds of the lighting technicians of the day. They represent in written form, if not always theories, the first extensive methodologies.

So let us pause here and compare our discussions so far with those of others.

BEGINNINGS OF THEORY

Who put pen to paper first is a little difficult to ascertain. In his notable book of 1970, Richard Pilbrow[1] describes Stanley McCandless in the US and Geoffrey Ost[2] in the UK as being the first to put forward '"the method" [which] suggests a basic formula for setting about lighting a scene and, as such, provides an excellent framework'.

The McCandless book *A Method of Lighting the Stage*[3] dates from 1932, and Pilbrow may well be right about his unifying approach, however by this time several other authors were also already in print. The Ost book was not published for a further twenty-five years.

Early Works
The Lighting Art[4] by M. Luckiesh was published in 1916, *Stage Lighting for 'Little' Theatres* by C. Harold Ridge[5] in 1925, and *Theatre Lighting* by Louis Hartman[6] in 1930.

Long out of print, I have none of these books before me. Interestingly, however, they are all included in the bibliography of *Stage Scenery and Lighting* by S. Selden and H.D. Sellman[7] published in 1930.

I do have a copy of Ridge's later book *Stage Lighting* that may well have been a refinement of the earlier one and was in its second edition by 1930. Another early author was Theodore Fuchs, whose book *Stage Lighting*[8] was published in 1929. If not exactly inventive in their titles – a problem that naturally only gets more acute with time – all these early books warrant our investigation.

Many of the first books on the subject deal rather obliquely with stage lighting. No one at that time had thought to arrange the relevant information into a method or scheme. These texts thus more often deal descriptively with

the equipment and its uses, recounting what is done rather than why. This is not really so surprising as in 1930 the term 'lighting designer' had yet to be coined.

What follows is an attempt to give a flavour of some of these books. In quoting from them it is interesting to note the similarities and differences between then and now – that is, between the theatre world when electricity was still an infant and our own, seemingly, highly sophisticated era.

STAGE LIGHTING, *C. HAROLD RIDGE, c.1930*
Ridge's book is generally 'descriptive' rather than theoretical. It does, however, allow us to establish a general context for all these early works. For example, Ridge lists available 'sources of light' as follows: Lime-Light, Arc-Lamps, Gas-filled Lamps, Vacuum Lamps and Special Lamps.[9]

'Types of lamp' are listed as Floodlights, Focus Lights, Spots and Projectors.[10] Both Focus and Spots are what we would now call profiles, with the latter differing from the former by being limited to a fixed focus.

It is interesting that even from the earliest days, quite sophisticated projectors had their place in the equipment list – projecting moving cloud effects and the like. Before their use in theatre, similar equipment had already become well established in the realm of the Magic Lantern Show.

In the chapter entitled 'Principles of Stage Lighting' Ridge starts by saying that, with the advent of 'modern equipment', the footlight was no longer relevant but had remained 'probably because no one had thought of doing anything else'.[11]

He says that 'in the very early days it was impossible to avoid ugly shadows on the stage … at the present day the general practice is to work with a shadowless stage for most general scenes'.[12]

This fascinating illustration (*below right*) shows how much *total* wattage would be expected on any particular part of the stage,

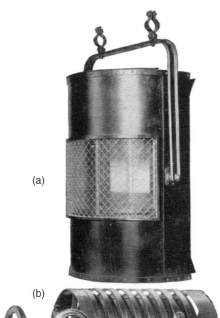

(a)

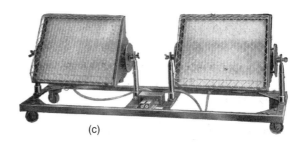

(c)

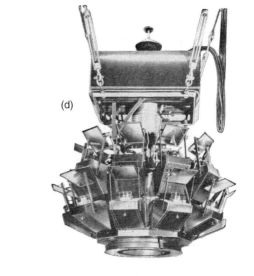

(d)

(b)

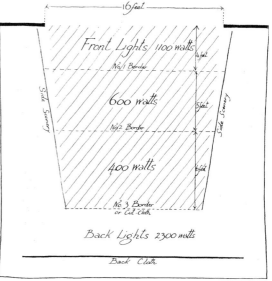

ABOVE: *Early lighting equipment.*

(a) G.E.C. 3000 watt Horizon Lantern with Colour magazine and Mechanical Dimmer.
(b) G.E.C. Control Regulator for operating a battery of 3000 watt Horizon Lanterns with Colour magazines.
(c) G.E.C. Mobile Ground Floods.
(d) Type W.O. 20. G.E.C. Cloud Apparatus with 20 projection systems arranged in two tiers. Designed for use with 3000 watt Osram gas-filled class A.2 Projector type lamp.

Ridge's ideal total wattages used on stage – 1930.

16 feet

Front Lights 1100 watts   14 feet

No.1 Border

Side Scenery

600 watts   5 feet

No.2 Border

Side Scenery

400 watts   6 feet

No 3 Border
or Cut-Cloth

Back Lights 2300 watts

Back Cloth

91

and demonstrates how little light was used in this period.

Interestingly, this was, of course, a still greater level of illumination than had previously been the case. In fact one of the more obvious factors in the whole history of theatre lighting is the progressive increase in the power of the instruments, and thus the potential increase in light levels on stage.

Finally, on colour, Ridge has this to say: I condemn the use of coloured light merely to gain a pretty effect. Coloured light should ... represent the light of nature, and/or ... aid the atmosphere of a play.[13]

A METHOD OF LIGHTING THE STAGE, STANLEY MCCANDLESS, 1932
This book, as its title suggests, follows a more methodical approach than that of Ridge. Here are the more relevant quotes:

The 'method' does imply the objectives of control – the regulation of intensity, colour, distribution and movement.[14]

Visibility, naturalness, composition, and atmosphere are the objectives for lighting – (It) vitalizes a plastic picture with lights and darks, deep shadows and glaring highlights if desired as no other medium in design can provide – in its brightness and darkness, its color and pattern. It creates an atmosphere that is inherently dramatic ... Light is a sense (that) provides a new horizon for artistic expression.[15]

The primary function of lighting is to give visibility.[16]

McCandless envisages three sets of equipment; one set to

divide the general acting area into a number of sections (generally six) ... Another set of instruments must be used to create motivating light ... and still another to provide the light distribution on the scenery.[17]

The diagram (opposite) shows how such equipment would be usually distributed on a medium-size stage: 'cross lighting is used on each acting area, to provide plasticity and proper visibility to the actor's face'.

McCandless also talks of colouring these units in keeping with their direction: 'those instruments focused in a direction ... will normally be of the same color', adding that 'if warm color is used from one side, cool color can be used from the other'.[18]

Of historical interest is his note that:

As long ago as the Renaissance it was discovered that the best balance of light and shade to promote the effect of plasticity could be obtained by considering sunlight falling diagonally, from over one shoulder.[19]

This leads him to comment that 'Plasticity is best achieved when the distribution of light is at 45 degrees in plan and elevation.' He then goes on that 'as a result it has been found wise to light each area from two diagonals with respect to the direction in which the audience are facing.'[20]

This last point will become possibly the most important philosophy of stage lighting, and one we have to return to in discussing the concept of a 'general cover' in the second part of this chapter (see page 96).

Before leaving McCandless we cannot, of course, fail to note that he also saw footlights as 'essentially artificial in their effect'.[21]

STAGE LIGHTING FOR AMATEURS, PETER GOFFIN, 1938
This book includes many fascinating elements new to the arguments of stage lighting, including a section on theorist Appia, George Fuchs and Craig.[22] But despite this, Goffin fails to describe a working method as clear as that of McCandless. In comparison his book, even in 1938, was 'a little behind the times'.

McCandless's layout for a medium-size stage – 1932.

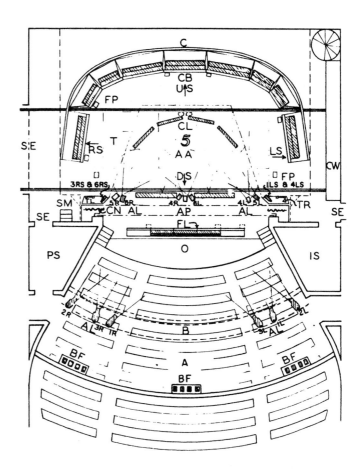

Of most interest are Goffin's comments on plasticity. Indeed he could perhaps claim to have been the first to use the phrase 'flat lighting', writing 'that lighting which gives solidity and life to a scene is called plastic lighting; when it fails to give the quality, we call it flat'.[23]

Finally, in a similar vein to those above, two wonderful illustrations are shown from *Stage Lighting* by Geoffrey Ost.[24]

Later Books

Each generation has sought its own books of reference and in recent years the expansion in the field of training in this area has meant a corresponding glut of lighting manuals. However, several key volumes are worth mentioning as they hold, or held, a key place in the market.

STAGE LIGHTING, *FREDERICK BENTHAM, 1950*[25]

The British lighting manufacturer Strand Electric (founded in 1914) was for many years the leading company in its field. In an ever-competitive and growing market, Strand has continued to hold its place amongst the best.

For many years, Strand was under the direction of Fred Bentham who led the development of many innovative lighting instruments. Bentham's book displays his infatuation with equipment and unfortunately is less informative about lighting design techniques or

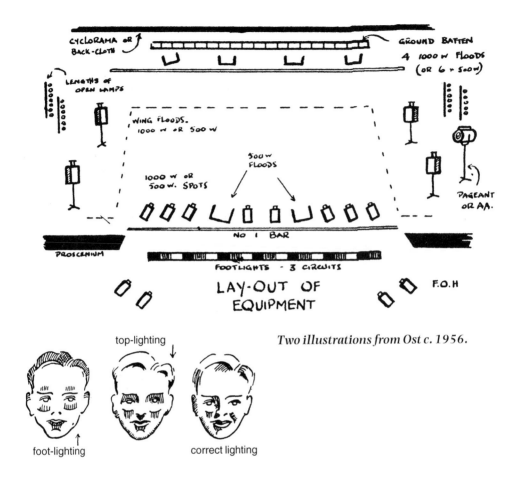

Two illustrations from Ost c. 1956.

theories than others in the field. Where it does prove most instructive is in the breakdown of the equipment, much of which, of course, he helped to design.

Fascinatingly, the book also goes into great detail about another interest of Bentham's – *Colour Music* – the idea of creating a visual performance of changing light set to music and projected onto an abstract three-dimensional stage setting. An art form ahead of its time, and one that perhaps reached a mass audience in the more abstract parts of Disney's wonderful *Fantasia*, and finds a smaller appreciation in modern video art.

The work of Bill Viola exemplifies this latter art form. His exhibition of summer 2001 'Five Angels for the Millennium and Other New Works' described thus: 'shafts of light slant downwards through the water, bubbles rise, sun is reflected on ripples. Then there is a swirling like a galaxy unfolding in space'.[26]

Bentham's interest in what he calls 'light as art' did inspire many later lighting designers and meant that Strand came to produce possibly the most user-friendly and flexible lighting controls. Although, admittedly, Bentham's first dalliance with the use of an organ console to 'play' lighting looks enormously daunting today.

STAGE LIGHTING, *RICHARD PILBROW, 1970*
Richard Pilbrow, who founded the company The-atre Projects in the 1960s, could be said to have written the first 'modern' book on stage lighting. It is still available and in his expanded version, *Stage Lighting – the Art, the Craft, the Life* (1997), covers more ground than any other.

In his original book Pilbrow expands on the method. He describes the properties of light as 'Intensity, Colour, Distribution, and Move-ment'.[27] Also he breaks down 'the objectives of stage lighting (into) Selective Visibility, Revela-tion of Form, Composition, and Mood'.[28]

Pilbrow's book is also greatly valued as it con-tains detailed technical specifications of most available lighting instruments – beam angles, and so on. These details would otherwise have to be obtained from each manufacturer or gleaned from a range of hire companies.

THE STAGE LIGHTING HANDBOOK, *FRANCIS REID, 1976*
Francis Reid has produced a cannon of work over the years, starting with this 'handbook'. For lucidity and a 'down-to-earth' approach Reid cannot be beaten. His book on the aes-thetic and actuality of being a lighting design-er, *Lighting the Stage*[29] is also superb.

In his book, Reid is being deliberately provoca-tive in defining stage lighting as 'a fluid selective atmosphere dimensional illumination appropri-ate to the style of a particular production.[29]

In the 'handbook', Reid also gives the clear-est (up until then) understanding of the posi-tioning of lanterns within 'the method' and, as part of this, the need to break down the stage into sections. In this context the concept that I have called 'parallelism' is also finally described with great clarity (*see* overleaf).

More Recent Books
To the connoisseur, all the books available today are of interest, and from Bentham onwards those above are also available in new editions.

To those wishing to learn, however, some texts are better than others – and in the Eng-lish-speaking world whether the book is meant for the European (often British) or the American market is particularly relevant. There are no fundamental differences between the US and the UK in terms of theory, but nev-ertheless the equipment available in each and the working practices do differ sufficiently to make it worth checking which you have before you.

The Further Reading section on page 155 contains a full range of books that I would recommend.

Of those who put pen to paper before the close of the twentieth century I would mention John Williams and Tim Streader's book *Create Your Own Stage Lighting*,[30] and Nigel Morgan's book *Stage Lighting for Theatre Designers*.[31] The latter was written by the deviser of the first degree courses in theatre lighting design in the UK.

My own earlier book *Lighting and Sound*[32] covers the two technical disciplines in detail, and perhaps could be said to finally confirm the concept of 'parallelism'.

It is also important to check these books for the number of practical examples and clarity of illustrations. Check that the text is readable and deals with the subject in depth rather than with superficial knowledge. For a real 'hands on' guide I would also recommend my book pub-lished by Crowood Press *Stage Lighting Design – a Practical Guide*.[33]

IN PRACTICE

The study of the books catalogued above shows us that if any part of the process of lighting a play can be said to follow a formula, it is that of covering the stage with general light.

The rest of this chapter seeks to sum up what we have learnt from McCandless onward about 'the method' and the 'general cover', starting with the concept of 'parallelism'.

PARALLELISM AND THE 'GENERAL COVER'

Parallelism is the notion that when building a 'general cover' using 'the method' – dividing the stage into areas and addressing each one separately – what is being strived for is defined as follows. If a group of lanterns is used to create the appearance of a single light source, then lines drawn along the centre of their beams would be parallel to each other.

This formula allows a lighting state to be created with any number of (apparently) different single light sources – the rules apply equally to front light, top-light, side-light and so on. They provide the appearance of 'angle consistency' – that is, an actor moving from one area to another is always being lit by the same light sources.

The choosing of the size of the areas into which the stage is divided is a crucial factor here. As a beam of light radiates in the shape of a cone away from an instrument not as a straight line, there will always be some deviation from the desired angle of light across each area lit. If the stage is divided into areas that are too big, this deviation will become apparent as the actor crosses from area to area.

Parallelism is only part of the concept of 'the method', and only one method of lighting a stage – two others are worth noting.

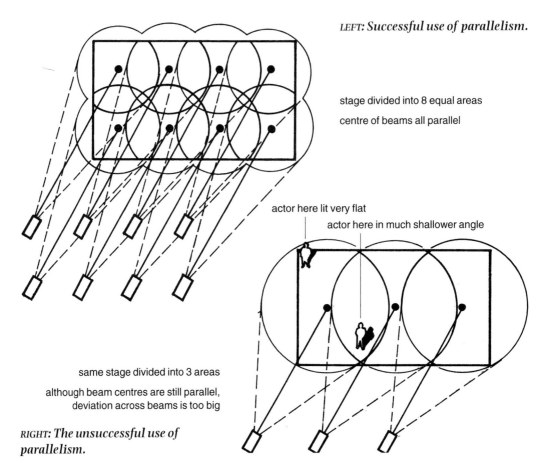

LEFT: *Successful use of parallelism.*

stage divided into 8 equal areas

centre of beams all parallel

actor here lit very flat

actor here in much shallower angle

same stage divided into 3 areas

although beam centres are still parallel, deviation across beams is too big

RIGHT: *The unsuccessful use of parallelism.*

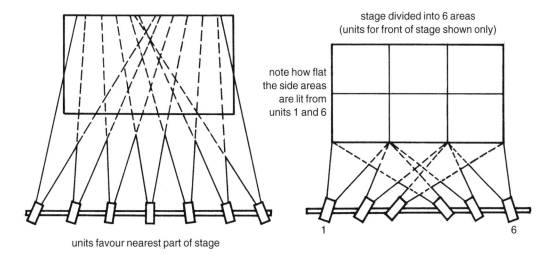

A lighting fan.

The early method.

The Lighting Fan

This concept uses electric equipment with much the same philosophy as those that preceded it – get the source as near as possible, but applied to units that do nevertheless project light and therefore may be rigged 'out front'.

In a 'fan', front light is positioned so that it favours the stage area nearest it (*see* above). As such, an actor walking across the stage will go through subtly shifting angles of light. In fact he will be generally flatter lit to the middle of the stage than the sides.

THE EARLY 'METHOD'

Pilbrow and others took the McCandless 'method', and adapted the 'fan' to provide less flat lighting, but they stopped short of 'parallelism'. *See* diagram above.

All three systems – 'fan', early 'method', and 'parallelism' – will work and may be applied to different productions, and in different theatre spaces.

'Parallelism' is perhaps the more modern, and the best way to echo the seemingly parallel

beams of sun or moonlight. The 'fan' gives a particularly interior quality. The 'early method', as I have called it, may be the best approach available in a theatre of restricted width. *See* the design example on page 145.

Having dealt with these variations on a theme let us now clarify what is meant by 'the method'.

'THE METHOD' – MODERN THEORY AND THE GENERAL COVER

What follows is my particular way of describing 'the method', and the illustrations incorporate the concept of 'parallelism' (*see* above).

Rules of 'The Method' (Diagrams A–J)

A. The stage area is divided into generally uniform areas.

B. Each area is addressed by lighting units in the same manner.

C. Any units that are lighting areas from the same angle can be thought of as a single light source, and are focused to overlap and blend together to achieve this.

97

a	b	c
d	e	f

NB: an odd number across allows a centre division

*ABOVE: **The stage divided. The Method – A***

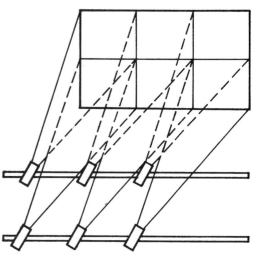

NB: *see* Parallelism, page 96

lanterns same distance apart as centre of areas

The Method – B.

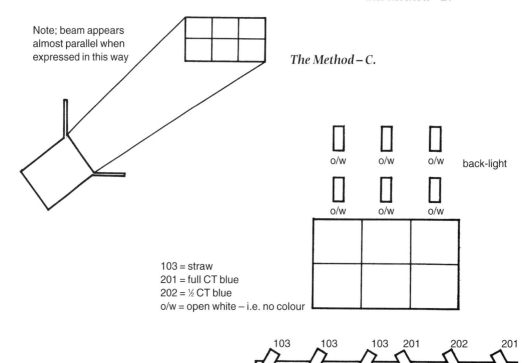

Note; beam appears almost parallel when expressed in this way

The Method – C.

o/w   o/w   o/w   back-light

o/w   o/w   o/w

103 = straw
201 = full CT blue
202 = ½ CT blue
o/w = open white – i.e. no colour

103   103   103   201   202   201

103   103   103   202   201   202

The Method – D.

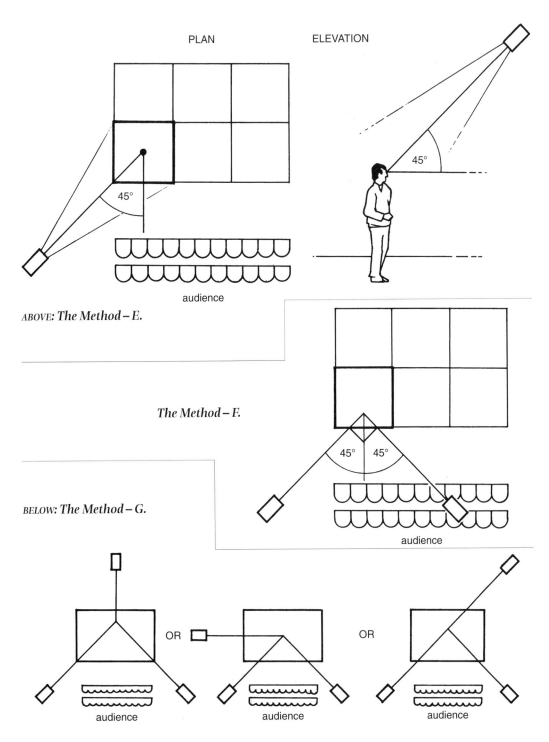

PLAN

ELEVATION

45°

45°

audience

ABOVE: **The Method – E.**

The Method – F.

45° 45°

audience

BELOW: **The Method – G.**

OR

OR

audience   audience   audience

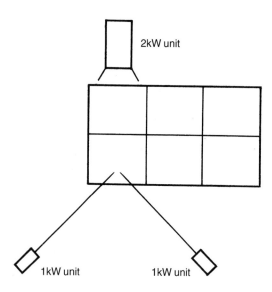

2kW unit

1kW unit   1kW unit

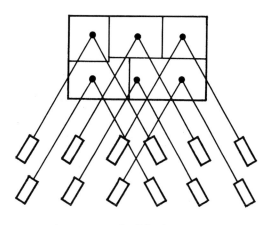

stage may need splitting into irregular
areas – i.e. as divided by the set or action

ABOVE: **The Method – H.**

RIGHT: **The Method – I.**

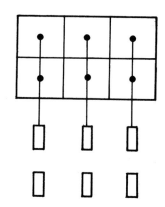

it may be easier to abandon certain
rules – here a single unit front cover needs
less equipment for front cover

D. Each light source should generally be of
    the same, or very similar colour.
E. For good actor visibility it is advisable to
    address an area with at least one unit at an
    angle of 45 degrees in both the horizontal
    and the vertical plane.
F. A second unit – at a 90 degree divergence
    from the first, but also as of E above, will
    maximize visibility.
G. A third unit is required to create plasticity
    and avoid flatness. This unit will come from
    an angle to the side or behind the actor.
H. The third light source (often back-light)
    should be at least as powerful as, or more
    so, than the combination of those facing it
    (*see* page 44).
I. It is not necessary to stick to the same form
    of 'the method' on each occasion – many
    variations are available.

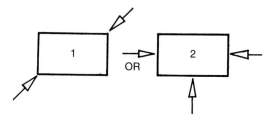

also light whole stage

The choice depends on the degree of naturalism and/or actor visibility required, and the style of the production generally.

J. To complete a design it is usually necessary to add specials, colour washes and set dressing as required. Always relating these back to your use of 'the method' in order to provide uniformity within the design – comparing your use of instrument, light output, colour, angle, and so on.

THE GENERAL COVER

The result of applying these rules is often described as a 'general cover' and can form the mainstay of any lighting design, often with little else needed to achieve a good end result.

Conversely, a general cover can be used simply to underpin a more complex design. Or, on rare occasions, may not be required at all, with specials and colour washes supplying all that is required.

What is important is to use 'the method' to facilitate a good design. That is, not just to create a general cover because actors need to be lit, but use it to add to the stage picture.

Colour or gobo a 'cover' to suit the setting; choose your angles and colours to describe the light sources that will serve the atmospheric needs of the piece; deviate away from a bland uniformity whenever the drama dictates it; use only parts of the 'cover' to underpin or supply specials.

CONCLUSION

The 'method' as described above was only really possible once reasonably powerful, directional and focusable units existed. This only occurred with the advent of electric light sources. After hundreds of years, it finally became feasible to light a stage without having to put the light sources as near as possible.

The footlight was finally to be consigned to the role of 'effect'. It would no longer be required to soften the harshness of inappropriate top lighting angles and provide front light. Theatre lighting could come out of the gloom of candle and gaslight, only choosing to create the atmosphere they engendered if required.

Instruments became available to allow us to create a light on stage that could go a long way to resembling the real light around us outside the theatre.

Coinciding with the historical push for Naturalism, followed by a backlash towards Expressionism, theatre lighting was able to respond accordingly. As part of this came the underlying thesis of most stage lighting; a means to address the stage – 'the method'.

'The method' gives the lighting designer one of their most powerful tools, and is generally indispensable in terms of achieving a good finished product, with good actor visibility.

It also provides a good starting point when building a design, and frees the lighting designer to concentrate on achieving total creativity.

Chapter Summary

- The creation of lighting theories derives from the introduction of electric light.
- General lighting of the stage is the dominant area in lighting theory.
- The theory of general lighting starts from simple principles.
- In practice, it is not necessary or desirable to adhere strictly to any particular theory of lighting.
- The importance given to the role of stage lighting grows with time and the increasing sophistication of control.

9 THE CREATIVE TEAM

The creative theatre process usually starts with the text. The creative team should know the text thoroughly in order to appreciate fully the possibilities of the piece, however the lighting designer should also be careful not to get too bogged down with the written word alone.

The play on the page is only a starting point. It is the director and set designer's 'take' on the text that really serves as the launching pad for the work of the lighting designer.

Often it is the play seen in rehearsal – a 'run-through' of the whole piece in particular – that most informs. For it is a 'run' that will more closely represent the look of the final production – not the play on the page.

The text may also indicate a setting; the time of day, the season, the weather conditions. It will also go a long way towards suggesting the mood or underlying theme of the production. However, texts are open to interpretation.

It is the interpretation of the mood of the whole play, or the scenes within a play that is a primary role for the director or designer. For it is up to them initially to create what we may call the 'production style'. How else does their work impinge on that of the lighting designer?

THE DIRECTOR

In the English-speaking theatre world, the role of the director is that of linchpin. The director is seen as 'auteur' or author of the piece. Directors are granted the role of the leader of a hierarchy that includes all the people working on

Meeting between Director, Designer and Lighting Designer – Karen Hebden, Neil Irish and the author – preliminary meeting for Letters to Felice *by Stephen Edwards.*

the production – performers, designers and technicians. Decisions may be taken at all levels, but the right of 'final say' on anything is given to the director. The only governing parameters that may thwart the director's ambitions will be those of logistics, time and money. Even then many a director will battle hard to stay even their potency.

Having given a lot of power to the director it is important that the director in turn learns to use it to the best ends – that he or she always aims towards the success of the production as a whole and not the needs of his or her own ego or reputation, or whatever.

Directors function best as inspirational guides to the team working 'below' them. Good directors put in an enormous amount of hard work and high levels of creativity themselves and, in the best sense, expect the same from those around them. They could be ultimately described as coercing, yet benign dictators whose aim is to seek collaboration not confrontation.

A few directors design or light their own productions, but none can contribute all the facets that make up a full professional piece. Theatre as most of us know it *has* to be seen as a collaborative art form. The best way for this to succeed is with directors who have strong ideas of their own, but also open themselves up to the ideas of others. They should work as a judge of and a filter to the ideas coming from the team around them, a team that provides technical and artistic answers, but also further challenges the ideas concerned with the work in hand.

The worst directors (to work for) brook no discussion, are not interested in any other opinions, function only to feed their own rather dubious needs, and generally behave like despots. They are frustrating and demanding in a way that is more likely to close the minds of those around them and generally stultify interest in the project in hand.

Somehow good productions can come from directors of either school, and all the variations in between. There is no doubt which type of director is the more enjoyable to work alongside, but sadly perhaps it is not nearly as clear as to which is the more likely to succeed or produce good work.

Personally, I believe that the former type of director is much more likely to have a higher strike rate. If they are good at what they do and surround themselves with other good people, staying open to influences and sensitive to the work of creating a production, the chances are

The Director – Nicholas Barter in rehearsal.

103

that they will produce fine work. Directors who work in a positive and collaborative way, in a manner that generally encourages people, are more likely to attract similar right-minded and talented people to work for them.

When working for a director on a project for the first time a lot of ground has to be covered, mostly in discussion, in order to establish the ground rules. Unlike a set designer, a lighting designer cannot present their work as a scale model. A lighting design plan says very little about what the lighting will look like. Lighting can only be described using words.

On a first project together, the leaders of the creative team (director, designer, lighting designer) will have to work hard to find means to describe what they are expecting of the lighting. Because of this, a team that works together on a second production will find it much easier to get their ideas to take off than may have been the case on their first production. If nothing else a great deal of trust will have been established, lessons learnt and working routines understood and set in place.

The director is often also the person who has the overwhelming ambition to put a particular play before an audience in the first place. This is not always the case but, even when play and director have been brought together by a producer or entrepreneur of some kind, it is still the director who must find the motivation to proceed. The director needs to make basic decisions about what the play has to say to an audience and how best to do this – their first ally in this process is the set designer.

THE DESIGNER

The designer needs to address and resolve a number of factors. Some are technical – for example, how many entrances or exits the set requires in order for the basic traffic of the play to proceed unhindered. Some are thematic – for example, what is the best way to show, in a visual manner, the basic underlying themes of the play.

In all, the designer has to integrate the technical and artistic issues inherent in the piece, and in the director's desires for the piece – that is, create a suitable three-dimensional world for the play to inhabit.

Thus it is the designer who has the job of interpreting the text and the desires of the director, to produce the overall look for the production. This resolves itself initially into a set model – a perfectly scaled (usually 1:25) representation of the look of the production, including how it may develop as the production proceeds on any given evening.

How the performers will look is also paramount. The look of the costumes is realized at an early stage, in this case as detailed costume drawings and sketches. Every costume for every character is shown, often with samples of the materials from which they will be made. The set designer and the costume designer are often the same person, but if not, will work in close collaboration at this stage.

THE PRODUCTION STYLE

The way the show will look, the themes that are inherent in this look, the interpretation of the concerns of the piece both visually (by the design team) and intellectually (by the director initially) combine to create the 'production style' for that production.

The same play produced by another creative team will inevitably have a different production style, and more than likely differ enormously in both look and feel.

If the director and designer are the traditional instigators of a production style, then the lighting designer is often their next port of call. Although on bigger productions the initial stages may well include producer, musical director, choreographer, and the author themselves (if the latter is living, of course).

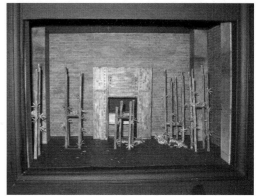

Four different set models for A Midsummer Night's Dream *– from the Rada Design Summer School (Designers: Michelle Reader, Clara de Sauvage, Susan Yeates, Thierry Cartoux).*

THE LIGHTING DESIGNER

The lighting designer can also be invited into the process that creates the production style, and therefore become involved at an early stage of the production process generally. Often, however, this does not happen. This may be for two reasons – one historical, the other logistic.

Historically, the trade concerned with creating the stage setting reached a much greater level of sophistication at a much earlier stage than the corresponding work of the lighting department. When lighting was still about trimming the wick, or even turning up the gas, the world of scenery was well advanced as the main creator of stage magic. In fact, the settings for many such performances could probably not have been bettered even with the hi-tech machinery we now have at our disposal.

The second point concerns the fact that, as the main purveyor of the stage vision, the designer has any number of seemingly impossible demands to reconcile. As we have discussed, these have come from the work of the

105

playwright and the director. The designer has to find a starting point, expand ideas, put them before the director, refine some, abandon others, and generally work through a very complex process before arriving at a final solution to the problems of the piece. As we have seen, this solution then defines the 'production style'.

To include the lighting designer, or anyone else, in this process can only be to add another raft of concerns, and inevitably slow things down before the larger team can meet to start work on the production as a whole. Thus the lighting designer (and others) are often only invited into the process at a point where the production style, and thus the set design, is nearing or has reached a final resolution.

This can be frustrating for the lighting designer, as a set designer will not always appreciate where the elements of the set may be most effectively placed, or coloured or textured, to allow the lighting to be at its best.

Some set designers do have this appreciation, but many do not, and thus it is better if the lighting designer is at least consulted at a point when the set is nearing consolidation but still remains potentially changeable.

As an intensely collaborative art form it can be seen that all the members of a theatre production team will impinge on the work of the lighting designer at some point in the process. It is therefore worth examining all the roles within a production, with attention to how they affect the lighting designer.

THE PRODUCTION MANAGER

The production manager is the person charged with overall responsibility for the technical and budgetary aspects of the production. They are concerned with safety issues, and oversee the project as a whole. They will chair the various meetings that involve the bulk of the production staff and will want to ensure that every

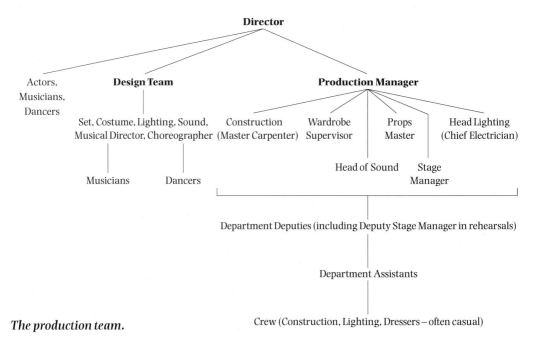

The production team.

department is clear about what they are going to contribute to the final production, what that will involve and how much it will cost.

The lighting designer will look to the Production Manager for information concerning the components of the job – ground plans and equipment lists may well be routed through or obtained from the production office.

Costings will go to, and budget allocations come from, the Production Manager. Work schedules, including the production schedule, will also come from the Production Manager. Here is the person imbued with the power to solve problems concerned with time, money, equipment and any other conflicts.

THE STAGE MANAGER

In charge of the stage management team generally, the SM will make sure that all the nuts and bolts of the running of the production, props and so on, are prepared and then run efficiently. The lighting designer may need the SM to help run stage electric cues efficiently – for example, smoke machines, stage practicals and so on, may be given to the SM team to operate and service. The Assistant Stage Manager and Props Dept also have a role in achieving this end.

The designer and stage manager (Gary Thorne and Sarah Tryfan).

THE DEPUTY STAGE MANAGER

The DSM is usually the person in rehearsals working alongside the director and cast. They are the fount of all knowledge concerning what the director is thinking and what the actors are doing. For the lighting designer they are also a good source of information about many things – for example, where the actors stand from moment to moment for certain scenes, what is changing in rehearsals, what the director has said about certain scenes, what is their mood or setting, and so on. As such, the deputy stage manager is a usually reliable source of detailed information about what the director may be thinking, and allows the lighting designer to check many aspects of the piece without bothering, or appearing to doubt or misunderstand, the director.

The DSM is also the person who cues the show in performance. They cue all the operators, including the lighting board operator and, where applicable, follow-spot operators and other technicians. The lighting designer thus relies on the skills of the DSM for the accurate placing and reproduction of cues. A sensitive DSM is one who can understand the reason for a cue so that it still fulfils its role as the play runs itself in from rehearsal through performance. As such a good DSM is worth their weight in gold (although unfortunately they are never actually paid this well!).

THE LIGHTING DEPARTMENT

A theatre lighting department usually consists of a head of department (traditionally called the chief electrician) and his deputies and assistants. A small department may consist of only one or two people and be additionally responsible for sound.

In some cases, the chief electrician may double as the lighting designer. If not, they are there to make sure that the lighting designer gets all the information and back-up required to complete the job successfully. Equipment maintenance, and rigging and operation will be their responsibility (*see also* page 150).

THE CONSTRUCTION DEPARTMENT

This department and the lighting team often share the stage – sometimes even crew members – it may also be the case that lighting equipment needs to be built in or around the set. For all these reasons, a good working relationship and communications are essential.

THE SCENIC ART DEPARTMENT

A good relationship with this department will help a lighting designer, who may well need to talk about the colouring and texture of a set.

The scenic art department can require a lot of time on stage to paint the set – the floor in particular is often painted on site – as such it is a good thing to be on good terms with the members of this department as you will often need to barter with them to achieve extra time on stage or to share the space with them at times during the production week.

The lighting designer may also want to take away any samples that have been made for the set designer and test colours on them in a workshop situation, and so again a good working relationship can help facilitate the cooperation needed.

THE SOUND DEPARTMENT

Sound equipment is often located near lighting equipment – access to it may also be shared. The sound being put together for a production may also impinge enormously on the lighting – whether music or effects. The timing, type, or mood of the lighting may need to be careful tied into the sound. Preview tapes may be essential.

Light Relief

Sammy Kahn, the song writer, when asked what is the starting point of the creative process that gets him to think of a new lyric was often quoted as saying: 'It starts with the phone call.' That is, however artistic the venture, the motivation can be somewhat more mundane.

As with all the departments mentioned above, it pays to understand the needs of others and cooperate so that they in turn will appreciate your needs.

CONCLUSION

Theatre is never the work of one person. It is not like purer forms of art where one individual can create a masterpiece alone – a painting or sculpture.

Very much like musical notation, the written word is only the beginning of the process. The interpretation placed on the work of a composer by a conductor or a musician is the same as the interpretation put on the work of a playwright by the director or performer. Unlike musical performance, however, a theatre piece requires the skills and creativity of more than just a sole interpreter or performer.

Without the production team, which places enormous technical knowledge and artistic judgement at the service of a dramatic event, there would be nothing.

This chapter has described the creative team and how it interrelates as it creates a piece of theatre. How the creative process actually functions in the department in the development of a lighting design and in the work of the lighting designer is the subject of the next chapter.

10 THEATRE PRACTICE

INTRODUCTION

Theatre spaces come in many shapes and sizes, from enormous opera houses to small fringe studios. In some cases the space is void of all technical equipment and *all* the lighting equipment needs to be imported: dimmers, controls, lanterns, rigging bars, and so on. At the other end of the scale, all equipment may be in place, lanterns rigged and focused and with no alterations allowed. Each extreme, and all the stops along the way, have their advantages and disadvantages.

PRE-PRODUCTION

Prior to the more intense sessions that inevitably precede the opening of the production is pre-production. This involves meetings, discussions, rehearsals, equipment preparation, hires, making and buying of equipment, and so on.

During this period, the lighting designer will work through a process of decision-making and selection to arrive at the necessary paperwork required to communicate all that will be necessary to prepare the lighting in the venue, up to the point where they will supervise the focusing. In particular, this process will result in the production of a drawn lighting design.

Perhaps the most important early meeting in the pre-production period is the Production meeting. In this meeting, the whole technical team (that is, everyone except the performers) discuss all aspects of the production. The director will put his concepts and ideas to the meeting, the set designer will often present a finished scale model of the set. All technical departments will be asked to comment, problems be discussed, and so forth.

The initial production meeting may be followed by any number of progress meetings – whatever is considered helpful to expedite and not hinder progress on the production.

PRODUCTION PERIOD (OFTEN 'PRODUCTION WEEK')

This period of intense activity sees the theatre in use almost constantly – often throughout the day and night, and at least for 12–14-hour day sessions. It runs from the 'get in' to the opening night, the work shifts/sessions attempting to follow a carefully planned 'production schedule'.

Get In

The equipment, costumes, and set arrive in the theatre. This is usually followed by the 'fit-up'. These are the sessions when equipment (particularly the set) is installed in the theatre space. For electrics, the major part of this is the rigging session.

Rigging

The lanterns are rigged and connected into the system, and pointed roughly in the right direction. Each lantern is usually hung from a bar or grid of bars. They may also be rigged on vertical booms or lighting stands.

Present Laughter

Directed by Robert Chetwyn

Designed by Peter Rice

Production Schedule

January 27th   Final Draft

Monday 31st of January
10.00 –0100 – LX and Construction load in at the
            BAC
01.00–02.00 – Lunch
02.00–06.00 – LX fit-up

Tuesday 1st of February
10.00–01.00 – LX fit-up Continue
01.00–02.00 – Lunch
02.00–06.00 – LX fit-up Continue

Wednesday 2nd of February
10.00–01.00 – Construction fit-up for the set
01.00–02.00 – Lunch
02.00–06.00 – Construction fit-up for the set
            Continue

Thursday 3rd of February
10.00–01.00 – Sound Plotting
01.00–02.00 – Lunch
02.00–06.00 – LX focusing

Friday 4th of February
10.00–01.00 – LX focusing Continue
01.00–02.00 – Lunch
02.00–04.00 – LX focusing Continue
04.00–06.00 – Scenic Painting

Monday 7th of February
10.00–01.00 – LX Plotting
01.00–02.00 – Lunch
02.00–06.00 – LX Plotting
06.00–07.00 – Dinner
07.00–10.00 – LX Plotting (with Director)

Tuesday 8th of February
10.00–01.00 – Start of Technical Rehearsal
01.00–02.00 – Lunch
02.00–06.00 – Technical Rehearsal
06.00–07.00 – Dinner
07.00–10.00 – Technical Rehearsal Continue

Wednesday 9th of February
10.00–01.00 – Scenic Painting
01.00–01.55 – Lunch
01.55–02.30 – The Half before the first Dress
            Rehearsal
02.30–05.00 – First Dress Rehearsal
05.30–06.55 – Dinner
06.55–07.30 – The Half before the second Dress
            Rehearsal
07.30–10.00 – The second Dress Rehearsal

Thursday 10th of February
10.00–01.00 – Technical time on Stage
01.00–01.55 – Lunch
01.55–02.30 – The Half before the first Dress
            Rehearsal
02.30–05.00 – Third Dress Rehearsal
05.30–06.55 – Dinner
06.55–07.30 – The Half before the Opening of
            Present Laughter
07.30–10.00 – The Opening of *Present Laughter*

Thank you

Anna Jordahl (SM)

Typical production schedule.

110

The lighting designer need not be present during rigging, although it can be useful to have them on hand if any problems arise. For the designer it can also be a valuable time in which to correct any minor faults that the placing of equipment may reveal.

Power is only put to the rig to check that all is working and properly connected into the system. Colour and gobos are usually put in place at this time.

Each lantern is connected to a dimming unit via a cable run, usually involving plug and socket connections.

The dimmer provides power to the unit and is remotely controlled by a lighting control board.

Units may be grouped together – paired – and connected to a single dimmer up to the power capacity of that circuit – that is, four 500W fresnel units could be paired onto one 2000W dimmer. In a case such as this, the control board would understand the group of four to be a single channel and thus any level set would apply to all four units. Independent control of each unit would only apply if each unit was connected to its own individual dimmer channel.

The control board uses a low-voltage analogue or digital signal to address the dimmers – that is, tell them at what 'level' to run the unit. Levels are typically described as being between 0 and 100 per cent, for example, 'Set channel 6 at 55 per cent'.

A typical studio theatre would have anything from twelve to eighty dimmers, a medium-sized theatre 80 to 120, a large theatre from 120 to 400, and so on. The lighting board would have the corresponding number of control channels, or capacity for more.

Rigging is usually closely followed by focusing.

Focusing

Once the lighting equipment has been physically installed – placed and connected to the electrical supply via dimmers and a control – focusing takes place. Focusing is the action of positioning the lanterns accurately to achieve the effect desired by the lighting designer, and required of the production in general.

Under the direction of the lighting designer, focusing is carried out in a total or near blackout so that the individual unit can be clearly seen. It is best carried out in a quiet theatre where the lighting designer can concentrate on what they are doing

The lighting designer will usually stand on the ground and direct a team of two or three who will carry out the actual manual work – focusing the lanterns, moving ladders, and so on. Focusing is covered in more detail in Chapter 12.

Parts of a typical lantern rig.

Plotting

Also sometimes called the lighting rehearsal, in this session director and stage management join the lighting team. Lighting states are created and designated cue positions in the script. Usually the deputy stage manager notes the cue positions in the master copy of the play – 'the book'. It is from 'the book' that the DSM will cue all departments in performance.

The lighting states are usually created in the order in which they will be used in the play – that is, starting at the beginning and working through to the end of the play.

Plotting is dealt with in more detail in Chapter 12.

The Tech'

The technical rehearsal involves working through the play with everyone involved. The cast practise their moves – it may be the first time they have been on the real set – and the technicians practise their cues. Sections of the play are rehearsed and replotted until everyone is happy that they are right. This can take some time – usually at least a long day, but possibly longer. Dress rehearsals follow.

Dress Rehearsals

A full run of the play as it will be in performance. There are typically three dress rehearsals.

Opening Night

The first performance to a public audience, unless preceded by 'preview' (try out) performances. The press are usually invited unless a later 'Press night' has been designated to allow the play time to 'settle in'.

Get Out/De-rig

Taking the set and all other equipment down and out of the theatre.

In lighting a production successfully, the lighting designer will need creative skills and artistry. However, just as the original design has required a detailed technical knowledge, so a lighting rig has to be installed and prepared efficiently and quickly in order to allow the designer to be free to express this creative side.

Inevitably there never seems to be enough time to do the job even when things do go well. If things are too long in preparation then time may seriously run out.

However well the lighting designer has prepared, the rigging and then the focusing must also succeed quickly in order that the lighting can be placed in the production with as much finesse as possible, so that the full creative/artistic worth of the lighting can be allowed to blossom. Efficient theatre work requires that the theatre space is sensibly used and that safe working practices, a methodical approach, planning, and good communications are applied at all times.

The paperwork generated or required in the pre-production period can give us a clue as to what this means.

Paperwork

An example of paperwork is shown on pages 114–15.

The Production Schedule

The timetable that everyone will be working to is called the production schedule (*see* example on page 110).

The production schedule comes from the office of the production manager (*see* page 106) and is usually negotiated with all departments before being finally confirmed.

Ground Plan

Either a) A scale drawing, in plan, of the theatre.

Or   b) A scale drawing, in plan, of the set superimposed onto a).

Theatre Electrics Layout (Circuit schematic)

The information concerning rigging positions, circuits outlets (sockets), permanent cable runs, and so on, usually superimposed on a) as above.

Equipment List

The list of which lanterns and other effects are available to the lighting designer. Careful attention is given to this so that the lighting designer does not use more equipment of any one type than is available (*see also* Drawing the Lighting Design Plan on page 128).

Circuit Fields

A list of the available dimmable channels.

Hire Source List

A list of items to be found, borrowed, hired or otherwise sourced. This could include extra lanterns, special effects, 'practicals' (electrics props that function as if real on stage – for example, table lamp, refrigerator).

Rehearsal Notes

These are produced by the stage management team (usually the DSM in rehearsal) and update the people outside rehearsals to requirements being suggested or implied as rehearsals progress. Similar notes will also be circulated from other meetings – the production meeting, or director/lighting designer discussions.

Focus Plot (Hook-up)

A detailed listing of what each lantern's role in the production is. This includes lantern type, colour/gobo, position in rig, channel/circuit/patch number, use, focus.

The focus is a description or picture of what the unit is lighting. This may be its role in the production or simply a way to identify how it is working – for example, a description of what part of the stage floor is incidentally lit when it is in the right position. This is particularly use-ful if a rig is being reinstalled, as when touring a production. In the latter case a stage cloth is often toured specifically marked up to aid such refocusing. The cloth is marked up as either a reference grid or a specific map of the focus for that particular show.

Patching Sheet

A means to notate which unit plugs into which outlet – in particular when a patching system is in use.

A *patching system* allows units to be re-allocated to dimmers whilst the show is running or at a convenient time – for example, the interval. It allows the lighting designer to rig more units than dimmers, and involves the lighting designer having to identify a number of units that are never in use at the same time.

Colour Call

A list of all the colour (gel) that is required listed with their relevant frame sizes, and so forth.

Lighting Plot/Cue Synopsis

A description of the lighting cues that will be created at the plotting session. A means to communicate what the plans are for the lighting in a given production.

Plotting or Cue Sheet

Information generated from the plotting session onwards that describes what the lighting board operator has to do to run the cues. It may include a description of the cues and their place in the production so that the operator can more easily identify an error in performance.

Electrics Running Plot

Information generated from the plotting or tech' sessions onwards that describes any cues that need to be carried out by the stage electrics staff – for example, smoke machine operation, follow-spotting and repatching.

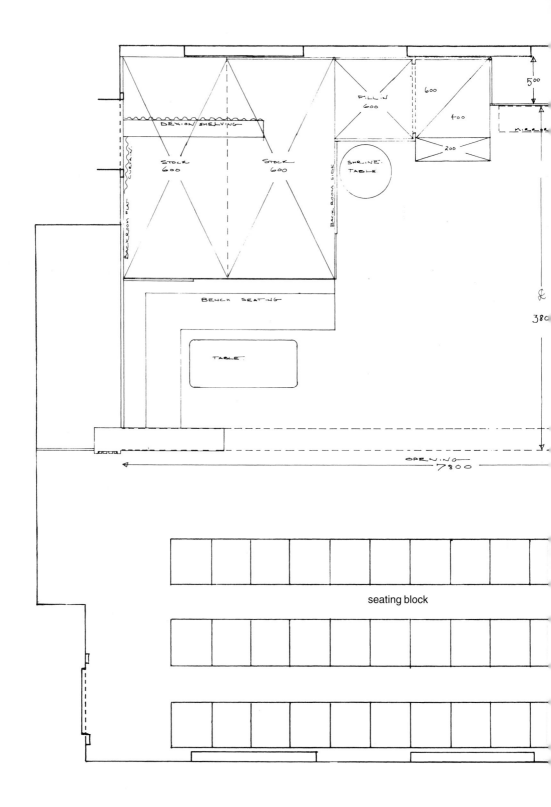

DEXION SHELVING

STOCK 600

STOCK 600

BACKROOM FLAT CURTAIN

BACK ROOM SIDE

FILL-IN 600

600

400

200

500

MIRROR

SHRINE TABLE

BENCH SEATING

TABLE

OPENING 7800

380

seating block

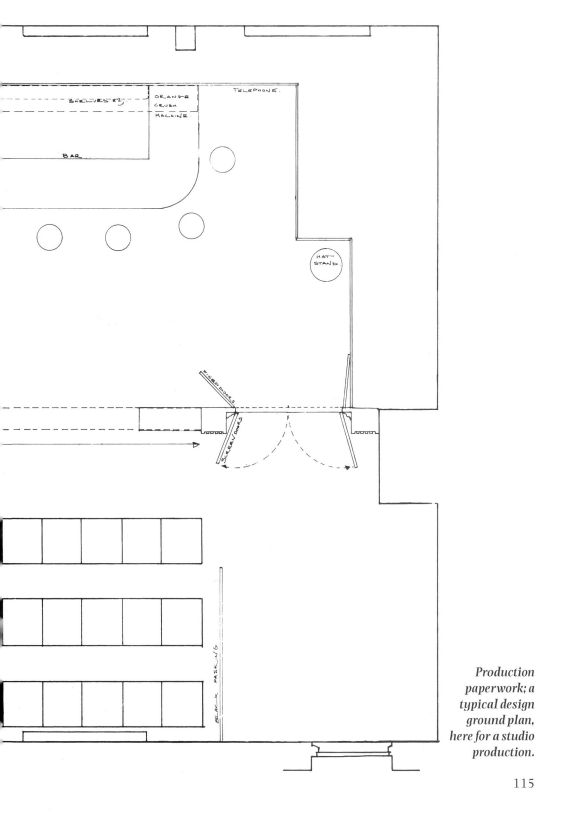

Production paperwork; a typical design ground plan, here for a studio production.

115

Lighting Design

A scale drawing, in plan, that carries all the information that the rigging crew need to put the lighting equipment in place and in full working order – this is, properly connected.

The 'plan' may also include notes that the lighting designer has made so that they can remember the focus of any particular unit. It will not afford enough information for anybody other than the lighting designer to focus the rig.

Although an experienced hand may be able to make a good guess as to what the lighting intention is by looking at the lighting plan, nevertheless the lighting design remains, in essence, in the lighting designer's head until after the plotting session.

All the paperwork described above plays an important role in the creative process of the lighting designer's work. Additional paperwork, which impinges even closer on this process, is discussed in the next chapter.

CONCLUSION

A well-organized, systematic approach to the work involved in the production process allows a production to really take off. A piece hampered by too little time and energy will not be as likely to succeed.

Good communications, early recognition of the needs of the production, good updated paperwork, well-maintained equipment, efficient rigging and focusing, capable lighting board operation and cueing, all of these are necessary to bring about a smooth transition from plan to stage, from thought to action, from text to performance.

11 THE LIGHTING DESIGNER'S PREPARATION

INTRODUCTION

In order to produce the lighting for a particular production, a lighting designer will have to gather relevant information, process it, and then make a number of informed decisions. By necessity this will have to happen before the set or lighting is put into position, and this period is called pre-production. The production period usually refers to only the part of the process when the team actually has access to the stage space.

Every lighting designer will gather information in their own particular way. Therefore what follows seeks to illustrate a basic working method. This has been proved to work well over time, and using this method an individual can seek to create their own particular style. It is an *approach* to the creative process rather than a definite answer.

A lighting designer will probably also have different ways of working dependent on the material they are working on – the type of production, the size and make-up of the team, the time scale involved and the budget. Every production has its own unique constraints and freedoms.

What follows, then, is a basic approach, a starting point, a general guide to the whole process of lighting a play.

READING THE PLAY

Read the play through carefully, making particular note of what each scene is saying about:

* *Location* – for example interior or exterior. Castle or cottage, England or Planet X.
* *Time Period* – day or night. Summer or winter. The hour of the day, sunset or sunrise, and so on.
* *Conditions* – sunny or rainy, warm or cold.
* *Specific Light Sources* – mention of fires, practical light fittings, a television, and so on.
* *Mood* – happy or sad, comic or tragic, tense or relaxed.

It may also be possible, even at this early stage, to begin to foresee where cues will be placed in the text. You may want to read the play through a number of times looking for each of the above on separate occasions.

It may be useful to start skimming through the text quickly, paying attention to the stage directions only, to ascertain a number of the more basic of the above, before undertaking a detailed reading looking for the emotional mood of each part of the play.

Again, even at this early stage, it is a good thing to start to visualize ideas about the way the piece may look – but do not get too stuck into any specific idea before seeing a set model or talking to the director or designer.

Director, Deputy Stage Manager and Lighting Designer meet to discuss cues (Nona Shepphard, Rachel Barkataki and Andrew Turner).

Keep your ideas free and relaxed, adaptable and easily disposable, if necessary. Also do not worry if little or nothing occurs to you at this stage – the text of a play can remain very cold on the page – inspiration may well come from the input of others.

MEETINGS AND DISCUSSIONS

Take your own ideas into meetings (it is good to prove that you are beginning to formulate ideas) but more especially listen to those of others. Note down all the technical information that is going to affect your work, and pay particular attention to the 'production style' being described by the director and designer.

In the big meetings with probably the full technical team (for example, the production meeting) confine your questions to those that affect the greater group. Arrange for smaller meetings with the director and designer (singly or together) to discuss the lighting requirements in detail.

Make sure everyone knows what you are expecting from various members of the team, especially if anything varies from the normal flow of things.

In the Production Meetings you will ask questions such as:

'Is the lighting going to need fully masking out?' that is, the light sources being hidden from the audience.

'Is that cloth on the set model being painted (as it is on the model) or will it be a real cloth?'

'Is the designer aware that the lighting rig (not shown on a model usually) will partly obscure a set piece?'

'Will the musicians need illuminated music stands?'

(to the director) 'When are you likely to reach a stage when I can see a "run" (of the play)?'

Make statements that give useful information, such as:

'We hope to be using two follow-spots, placed on the circle front.'

118

'There will be a smoke machine in use stage left.'

Do not look for conflict, take serious problems to the individuals concerned or through the production manager. Generally try and think through the repercussions of all that is being said. Certainly do not take anything for granted – especially the needs of the director. Make good notes of anything that you may wish to refer to later.

Anything that will specifically impact on the budget may require careful handling and may also need a separate negotiation with the production manager.

MEETING WITH THE DIRECTOR

As with all meetings, the art is to *listen* and *understand*, to make your own points and explore ideas.

The director may want to talk to you at an early stage of the rehearsal period or even prior to it, or they may be happy to wait until much later. Likewise you may value an early meeting or prefer to wait until you have seen some rehearsals. Whatever the case, do not be pushed by the production process into a meeting that neither you nor the director really wants. If nothing has been said when you need information from the director, ask for a meeting yourself – do not be shy about this.

In meetings with the director, a number of issues may need to be resolved. If nothing else, the scope of the production and the manner in which the director likes to use lighting need to be ascertained. Along with this will come a general sense of how much freedom the director is likely to give you in the making of artistic decisions. As discussed previously (*see* page 102), some directors will take charge – dictating many aspects of the lighting, even down to the choice and positioning of equipment, whereas others will give a very free hand to the lighting designer.

Some directors will seem to have almost no idea about what they want, or certainly poor skills in communicating their ideas. Considering the amount of preparation that can go into a lighting design and the lack of time once in a theatre, one of the worst comments that can be made by a director is: 'I cannot really say what I like, but I will know it when I see it' ... especially when it is followed in time by 'No, that's not it.'

Generally directors give one enormous gift to the lighting designer – one that being so commonplace can easily be forgotten or ignored, it is this.

Unlike the set designer, a lighting designer cannot make a scale model of what the lighting is going to be like. It is only at the 'plotting session', after an enormous amount of time and effort has been spent on the lighting, that the director begins to see what has been in the lighting designer's mind for weeks. At this point the director cannot really say 'Oh, no, that is not what I want at all.' Their gift is to understand that at this point what they have to do is begin to see their production within the parameters of what the lighting is providing. They can say 'Can the lighting be brighter or a different shade?', they can ask for a new lantern or lanterns to be rigged to do something new, they can ask for any large or small variation on what they are seeing *but* generally they must be prepared to accept the overall mood that the lighting designer has worked painstakingly to create.

It is thus supremely important that the lighting designer creates a lighting rig that functions to solve the problems of the play, creates the right moods, and is obviously seeking to aid all that is going into the production. The importance of good preparation, including good communication with the director, is thus paramount.

When talking to the director, the answers to some of the following questions may help, especially at an early stage, to get you thinking in the right direction:

119

'Do you foresee a lot of cues within each scene, or do you think it is basically just a change of light for each scene?'

'Do you like to plot each cue very accurately or are you happy to bash out a basic plot in the lighting session and refine it later in the tech?' (technical rehearsal).

'What underlying mood do you think the lighting/play/scene/act should have?'

'What do you want from the lighting?'

Of course with many of these questions you may have an answer you want to hear – a way in which you like to work or an idea about the production. In this case, phrase your question accordingly:

'I see the play as gradually becoming darker and darker in mood. Do you think the lighting should generally echo this?'

'Would you like to keep this piece within the constraints of quite a limited use of colour in the lighting?'

I don't think the lighting for this play needs to be over-colourful, does it?

'I see this as a warm upbeat piece and it would seem to make sense that at no time should we actually fade to blackout, but rather cross-fade straight in and out of scene changes. What do you think?'

and so on ....

SEEING A RUN

Sooner or later you should be able to see a 'run' of the play in rehearsals. Directors will often refer to their first run as a 'stagger through' but actually for the lighting designer it is often as good as the real thing. The first run is so near to the rigging session anyway that it is often the only 'run' that the lighting designer will see that will still allow time for the lighting design to be thought through and designed.

In a first run there will, in any case, be most of the aspects of the production that the lighting designer requires to know. Nearly all the aspects can certainly be gleaned from even the most poorly acted rehearsals.

When going to see a run it is important that the lighting designer is properly prepared. Take into the 'run':

* Notebook and pens (keep spares handy), or write alongside the text in the script itself.
* The script – it is often useful to keep an eye on how any moment fits into the scale of the whole production, and any unclear moments may need clarifying with a quick glance at the text.
* A sense of the set. Take in a ground plan or even the set model itself if it is available, and put it where you can see it during the 'run'.

It may be useful to make sketches of the set and copy them so that you can use them to annotate moves or the settings for different scenes, and so on.

Remember to ask the director or DSM questions to help clarify what you are going to see:

'Is anything or anyone missing?'

'Is the set "marked out" accurately in the rehearsal room?'

'Is there anything I should know about this run that won't be true of the finished product?'

Get a good seat, perhaps close to where the bulk of the audience will sit. Do not be 'fobbed off' with a seat over to one side unless this is going to be helpful. Similarly do not allow yourself to feel too inhibited – move a chair to where you want it.

Choose to be near or far from the director and/or DSM as you wish. The DSM can be a fund of useful information – whispered during the run. As can the director. Or you may wish to be alone to concentrate on your work without interruption.

Get comfortable. It is good for the lighting designer to relax (as much as possible) so that the information and ideas can flow, allowing the imaginative juices freedom to interpret and respond to what is being presented. Not only visualizing how the production will fit into the theatre space that is being used and how best to light it on a technical level, but also allowing as much of a creative response as possible to stir the creative process. Make pictures in your mind and dress the 'run' in the 'clothes' of light appropriate to the piece

It may be ideal to see more than one run, and to be looking for different things on each occasion. It is, for example, not a bad idea to go to a run even after drawing up a lighting design to confirm the decisions taken still hold and do not need last-minute revision.

During the whole production process, the lighting designer is working through a process that seeks to combine the often seemingly disparate spheres of wild imagination and down-to-earth practicality. Fantasy meets technicality. Nowhere is this more acutely felt than at the moment, during a 'run', when inspiration has to be balanced with the rational.

So, during a 'run', let your imagination run riot but remember also to temper it with technical common sense. For example, no, you cannot arrange for the roof of the theatre to lift off and disappear for a highly climactic moment at the end of Act 3 – but yes, with the right equipment, you can make the same kind of impact (or nearly so)!

In a 'run', the lighting designer should make clear, precise and short notes. Do not spend your time looking at your notepad or the script and, in particular, pay attention to the following:

* Where are the scenes played? – that is, on what part of the set? Where do people stand? (Even, which way do they face?)
* What is the mood of each scene or moment of the play? How could the lighting best echo this?
* Does the mood shift dramatically? Should the lighting do so also?
* Where exactly do the lighting cues go? – write them alongside the text if possible with a brief descriptive note. This will be the basis for a cue synopsis (*see* page 123), and aid the following:
* Mood – for example, happy/sad, comic/tragic, tense/relaxed.

Be prepared to ask questions after seeing a 'run' but be aware that the director may have any number of other worries at this time – especially if they feel that what they have just seen was an unmitigated disaster! If you feel that this was the case do not even start to express this – be positive and supportive and leave your questions until a more suitable time.

PRE-PRODUCTION PREPARATION

A theatre lighting department (LX Dept) will have any number of things to do as a new production makes its way through the necessary processes before 'hitting' the stage. The lighting designer has to be aware that there is thus a need to fit into this process. This may involve having the answer to various questions within certain time constraints.

The LX Dept will need to service, stock, hire, borrow or make equipment as the production and thus the lighting designer requires. Usually as part of initial conversations, and in order not to be rushed later, it is worth asking the head of the LX Dept (usually called the chief electrician) when the finished lighting design on paper needs to be completed.

When working some distance from a theatre you will have to allow time for the lighting design plan to get to the venue in order to be checked by the LX staff. You may need to ask other questions about how you are to be involved – for example, will they circuit up the plan? Are you required to be on hand for the rigging session?

Other arrangements may be needed. Sometimes a touring production will come with its own equipment. But it may be that in-house team supplies colour and/or gobos.

Whatever the case, the lighting designer must retain a good overview of the whole process. They are not expected to do all the lighting work (well, not often, anyway!) but it is foolish for a lighting designer to put in hours of creative work only to turn up to the venue to discover that some fundamental part of the lighting rig is not achievable because no one knew about it.

It must not be forgotten that whilst working through the pre-production period described in this chapter, the lighting designer is still applying a creative mind to problems and ideas that are being presented to them – whether from reading the text, talking to others, listening in meetings or watching rehearsals.

The solutions that the lighting designer finds to these stimuli will be derived from their individual understanding of how light works on stage – an understanding derived from the ideas that we have discussed in the earlier chapters of this book concerning form, shape, movement, colour and mood.

Paperwork

As we have seen in the previous chapter, the need to process and evaluate a certain amount of paperwork is a requirement of the lighting designer's job.

Remember that the point of this paperwork is to help the lighting designer keep track of what they are doing, and communicate clearly with the rest of the LX team, and others.

All the listed items in the last chapter have a part to play in the lighting designer's preparation. Let us now revisit some of them from this perspective.

Rehearsal Reports, Calls, and so on

The director and actors in daily rehearsal are joined by the DSM, who writes up a daily bulletin concerning what has developed in these rehearsals – a 'rehearsal report'.

For the lighting designer, this may include information about things the director has said in rehearsals like 'There will be a lighting cue here to allow for the scene change' or 'You will be in a special for this part', or 'We will close down to the fore-stage at this point', or 'You will be in a follow-spot for this speech', or 'There will be a light switch there.' Much of this may simply confirm previous discussions but some of it may require new ones!

There will also be paperwork confirming what part of the play is being rehearsed when (call sheets). The 'call sheet' will allow the lighting designer to visit rehearsals for specific parts of the play that they need to see. The placing of the actors within a scene – where they will stand at any given moment – is something that the directors and actors may work out early on in rehearsals or not. This is called 'blocking'. The director may know his mind, in this area, from the first day. Whatever the case, a visit to rehearsals can be useful to get the tenor of the production.

The Production Schedule

Time is often at a premium once the theatre has closed down to allow a new production to be mounted, so it is necessary for the lighting designer to make sure that they have enough time to get the work done within the planned schedule, and scale the work accordingly. When the schedule is presented in its initial form the lighting designer must be skilled at knowing if the time they are being offered is enough, and at negotiating for more.

It is also worth developing the skill to see better alternatives on a plan and problems that might arise. For example a lunch break may not be really necessary if the two teams working before and after the break come from different departments – for example, construction crew and LX crew. It makes no sense for the theatre to be empty in between sessions – rather that they have different lunch times – for example, one team could have an early break and start as the other team finish.

Likewise, a paint call in a morning makes no sense as paint will need to dry before the stage will be accessible – better that this call should finish the day, and so on. *See* the example of a production schedule on page 110.

Light Relief

Lighting designers are often very reluctant to finally put ink on paper, or manipulate the first icon on a CAD screen. There is a distinct feeling that once they start there will be no turning back – any wrong decisions will be irretrievable.

With students I feel I often have to bully them to get on with the process:

'Look', I say, 'there are millions of places your first lantern could go – the possibilities are endless – how can you possibly be expected to get it right – it is not the issue. Just remember that unless you get your drawing finished in good time, you will never have the time to go back, check and revise, and finally see why that first unit was wrong'.

A Cue Synopsis/Lighting Plot

A cue synopsis, or lighting plot, is a useful device to communicate or confirm the contribution being made to the production by the lighting. It may derive from meetings. It may be a communication from the director to the lighting designer, or vice versa. Either way it helps firm up ideas and avoid conflict later. A synopsis can be very detailed or quite basic (*see* illustration pages 124–5).

The process of putting ideas onto paper (*see* below) is not usually a straightforward one, and thus it is useful to keep an up-to-date check on what equipment you have used and which channels in the theatre space. As any are used they are crossed off the list – and if changes are made, the list is altered accordingly.

Developing an efficient routine using these aids can mean less embarrassing mistakes finding their way onto the finished lighting design plan.

Of all the pieces of paper involved in the process of lighting a show, the drawn lighting design is, perhaps, the most important document in the whole process.

THE LIGHTING DESIGN ON PAPER

The point of the process when ideas have to be finally committed to paper seems to hold a particular fear for many lighting designers.

The first thing to be said is that there is no point in starting to draw a plan if you are not ready. Here is a check list to help you know when you can consider yourself at the point where you are ready to start drawing:

* Do you have all the relevant technical information – equipment, number of dimmable ways, rigging positions?
* Do you have the means to draw – paper, pencil, pens, eraser, stencils, computer program, peace and quiet, and so on?

LIGHTING CUE SYNOPSIS – 'YERMA' – Provisional

Preset – Set dressed – dark – House lights in

Q1	Start – Back Light on Actors increasing in intensity – oppressive – warm/white and hot. House out.	
Q2	Build further as rig slowly descends – change in song.	
Q3	Subtle build for Yerma down stage centre.	
Q4	End of first section Yerma down stage	Act 1 – Page 159
Q5	Possible change for Yerma – mid stage centre "Where have you come from, my love, my child?	– Page 161
Q6	Shift again as Maria enters	– Page 162
f/o Q	– Close down stage and increase oppressive feeling	
Q7	Subtle build or change for Victor scene	– Page 165
Q8	End of scene – Song	– Page 166
Q9	End of scene – transition to scene 2	– Page 166
Q10	Scene 2 – Slowish build to hot day	– Page 166
Q11	Slow darken to evening – '2 young girls come in'	– Page 170
Q12	Mood change and increase evening on entrance of Victor	– Page 172
Q13	Deepening mood – Yerma 'Listen'	– Page 173
Q14	End of scene – transition	– Page 174
Q15	Slow build to stylized scene on rock	Act 2 – Page 175
Q16	Further build as song starts	– Page 175
Q17	Build to full state – Bright cold mountain feel (After Song)	– Page 175
Q18	Possible change – colder – sisters-in-law enter	– Page 177
Q19	Possible cue – shift – 'I'll wash your ribbons'	– Page 178
Q20	Intensifying to end of scene 'Alas for the Barren Wife'	– Page 180
Q21	– transition – thru black or straight to chair	– Page 181
Q22	Build specials on sisters and Juan down stage	– Page 181
Q23	Build and break moment – 'You might as well lay the table' (specials out as sisters leave)	– Page 181
Q24	Subtle build special on sisters d.s.r. enter	– Page 181
Q25	Lose special as sisters exit	– Page 181

Typical cue synopsis – **Yerma** *by Frederico Garcia Lorca.*

Q26 Build white intensity during argument   – Page 182

Q27 Yerma on rock – change to stylised red sunset 'Oh field of sorrow'   – Page 184

Q28 Possible build required – Maria enters   – Page 185

Q29 State darkens – 'That's a terrible thing to say'   – Page 186

Q30 State darkens more – sister appears with bread   – Page 187

Q31 State darkens more – second girl enters   – Page 187

Q32 Possible change – Victor enters – moon/light   – Page 187
     Sun continues to set thru – thus sisters in silhouette for Page 189

Q33 Darkens to very dark on stage for end of Act 'Yes lets go'   – Page 190

Q34 d.b.o. end of Act   – Page 190

Q35 Scene 1 – Night – dark   Act 3 – Page 191

Q36 Sun begins to rise – glimmer   – Page 193

Q37 Continue build faster to suggest tension – Juan enters   – Page 194

Q38 End of scene – transition   – Page 196

Q39 Beginning of scene, procession across. Dark.   – Page 197

Q40 Slight build for Pagan Woman scene   – Page 197

Q41 Possible further subtle build for First Girl   – Page 197

Q42 Possible cue needed to accommodate candles – dim   – Page 198

Q43 Build on Yerma down stage   – Page 198

Q44 Snap out any extra candle light with snuffing   – Page 198

Q45 Carnival – introduction of subtle colour into the night (possible shifting during – i.e. several Qs)   – Page 199

Q46 Calmer state – night – From Pagan Woman lines   – Page 202

Q47 Closes down to Yerma and Juan (Pagan Woman goes)   – Page 204

Q48 Close down to special on Juan/Yerma 'I want you'   – Page 205

Q49 Water goes red   – Page 206

Q50 Rig and solo special fly out – cast enter   – Page 206

Q51 End – d.b.o.   – Page 206

Q52 Call

Q53 Postset plus House Lights.

✳ Do you know all there is to know about the setting – shape, placing, colour and texture of the set and costumes?

✳ Do you know what is expected of the lighting – from director, design and yourself? Do you know how to achieve it?

You may be most insecure about the final point. How do you know if you know enough? An effective and simple way to proceed is by making a needs list: a list of everything you need to make the lighting successful – most usefully, this list can in itself generate the drawn lighting design – as follows.

The Needs List

From the meetings you have had, from the ideas you have had on reading the text, seeing the set design model and costume drawings, and seeing a run, write a list of everything you think the lighting needs to do.

Blue colour wash for night
Specials: DSR
        DSL
        USC
        For speech on Page 6 (DSR)
Dressing on set
Specials on doors on set
Light behind entrances
Gobo wash to suggest creepiness
Gobo wash to suggest exterior – forest
General cover for the stage, for visibility, warm, day
General cold cover – cold day and moonlight

Then put this list in order of priority, and try to keep it on one side of a piece of paper so that things at the bottom of the list do not escape your attention.

General cover for the stage – for visibility, warm, day
General cold cover – cold day and moonlight

Blue colour wash for night
Gobo wash to suggest creepiness
Gobo wash to suggest exterior – forest
Specials: DSR
        DSL
        USC
        For speech on page 6 (DSR)
Dressing on set
Specials on doors on set
Lighting behind entrances

The prioritized 'needs list' is then merged with the 'equipment list', the lighting designer going through the list choosing the best equipment to use for each need. The thought process behind the prioritizing adheres to the following:

✳ Those needs that are essential to the success of the production come before those that seek merely to embellish – for example, the general covers that give visibility, and the required specials, except:

✳ A greater priority should be given to any lighting need that requires a number of units of a similar type to achieve it – rather than those that require only one or two units – for example, again the general cover but also the colour and gobo washes, however the specials move down the list on this count.

✳ Those needs that may seem to be defined as mere embellishment should not be undervalued where the success of any part of the play or its entirety will be greatly enhanced if they are included – again, the gobo washes, and the set dressing.

✳ Give least priority to design niceties that you can live without – the light behind doorways, and other enhancements of this nature.

These priorities will differ from piece to piece – on a naturalistic set, the light behind the doors may be thought of as a greater asset as it continues the sense of realism off-stage. On a non-naturalistic setting, however, the actors going off-stage into darkness may not be considered such a problem or even required.

As part of the decision process involved in choosing equipment, the lighting designer will eventually have to think of what equipment will be used. This can then be put on the list beside the needs (*see* illustration below).

The finished product is not arrived at as easily as described above. The lighting designer may have to revise ideas and re-prioritize. For example, initially it may have seemed preferable to have used all their profile lanterns on the general cover. However, when the need for the gobo washes is reached, a rethink becomes apparent. The list may have to be worked through a number of times before the best deal is done, and this can take some time.

Some experienced lighting designers successfully attempt this process whilst drawing up the design – stopping at each 'need' to evaluate it fully before drawing the relevant lanterns onto the design – but this is not for the faint-hearted as it is only too easy to 'paint oneself into a corner'.

Once this process has been completed, however, the 'needs list' becomes almost synonymous with the finished lighting design – but in a different form. All the lighting designer needs to do is work through the list and draw the equipment onto a plan in the positions also listed. At

Lighting Provision

NEED	UNITS	COL/GOBO
General cover for the stage for visibility, warm, day	12 × Sil 30	103
General cold cover – cold day and moonlight	12 × Sil 30	201
Blue Colour Wash for night	4 × 243	174
Gobo wash to suggest creepiness	12 × Cantata 11/26	o/w (dha 543)
Gobo wash to suggest exterior – forest	12 × Cantata 11/26	159 (dha 805)
Specials: DSR	2 × SL 15/32	212
DSL	2 × SL 15/32	212
USC	2 × SL 15/32	212
for speech on page 6 DSR	1 × P743	202
Dressing on set	6 × P743	009
Specials on doors on set	6 source 4	053
Light behind entrances	6 × Cantata F	061

Example needs list.

this stage the use of an equipment checklist and a circuit field is very useful as it avoids the possibility that the lighting designer may have used more equipment than is available or assigned the same circuit number twice.

Occasionally, colour is also chosen at this stage and written onto the 'needs list' – but the lighting designer can leave this decision as a rough notion only – warm, cold, blue, pink. The actual gel can be chosen after the rest of the drawing is done, thus adding this set of information as one of the last aspects to be put onto the plan.

Also last to go on may be the circuit numbers. They are more easily added by the head of the lighting team who knows the venue better and not by the lighting designer at all. The lighting designer may want to draw on where the numbers are to go, however – often as circles next to each unit.

For added clarity a lantern key is also drawn and any relevant notes (*see* illustration of finished lighting design on page 145).

DRAWING THE LIGHTING DESIGN PLAN

There are two main ways to realize a lighting plan – by drawing using pen or pencil or by using CAD (Computer Aided Design). In either case the fact that the lighting designer has started to draw does not mean that something cannot be changed – it is not uncommon to start a drawing several times having re-evaluated a major aspect of the design whilst thinking through the plan. Indeed when drawing up a plan, it is a good idea to check that your thinking has remained true to its aspirations, that too many compromises have not meant that the lighting is going to achieve very little impact where it should be greater, and so on.

Using conventional methods, it is sensible to draw the plan initially in pencil to allow for mistakes to be rectified and changes made.

It is not important that the finished lighting design be the most spectacularly smart diagram ever made (although work at this level is impressive), but rather that the plan communicates clearly to the LX team what the rig is supposed to be, and allows the lighting designer themselves easy access to the information on it. So, for example, labelling, numbering and instructions on the plan should be clear and unequivocal.

Stencils are available to aid the designer in drawing lantern symbols and as the rest of the design usually can be reduced to straight lines a very good-looking design is usually not too difficult to achieve, even without a computer.

Drawing the lighting design.

COMPUTER-AIDED LIGHTING DESIGN

CAD programmes do not make for better lighting designers but they can mean that the drawn design looks smarter (and is thus easier to use) and such programmes can also save time by generating much of the other necessary paperwork – equipment lists, colour calls, and so on.

Other lighting design packages can also allow the lighting designer to see in three dimensions what their design is going to look like in the theatre – especially in terms of what the beams of light will hit and how big and what shape they will be. They are particularly useful for automated systems (*see* Intelligent Lights on page 31) where the programming of moving lights can become very complex and it is useful to have pre-programmed many (if not all) aspects of their use prior to their actually being rigged.

Software that deals specifically with theatre lighting design is available with varying levels of sophistication, depending on which manufacturer you visit. As these systems become progressively detailed there may come a time when the 'Holy Grail' of theatre lighting design is achievable: the ability to view and therefore refine a full lighting rig in all its complexity before actually installing it. Thus being able to call up any theatre stage from disc, install a set model – perhaps taken by computer from a ground plan and textured from the set designer's working drawings, people the stage with appropriately costumed figures and then install and play with a lighting rig to achieve maximum efficiency and optimum effect.

CONCLUSION

Good preparation and efficient working practices will mean that the lighting designer will be able to realize the full artistic potential of the lighting rather than remain strait-jacketed by the technical aspects of the job.

In this chapter a technique has been described to enable the lighting designer to get their ideas from page to stage. This can be seen again in Chapter 13, which presents a final example of the creation of a complete lighting design.

It is important that an economical and thorough working method is developed in this area. But, in what may appear to be a highly technical process, we must not forget that there has to be space for creativity. For without it there is really no design. The technical details are, after all, simply a means to an end.

Anybody can point light at an object and illuminate it – if nothing else, the whole point of this book is to show how there is so much more to be had from lighting a play than this.

The next chapters describe the part of the process when, after the detailed preparation described above, and after having installed the lighting rig into the theatre space, the lighting designer can once again engage with the more creative aspects of their role.

12 THE WORK OF LIGHTING

INTRODUCTION

It could be said that a lighting design is only as good as the preparation that has gone into it. However a good lighting design on paper can be ruined in the process of being translated from paper into reality and, conversely, a badly thought-through design can be rescued.

After the lighting rig has been installed, the real work of the lighting designer begins. These sessions, called focusing and plotting, are where the lighting is finally realized, and finely crafted.

FOCUSING

Focusing is the act of pointing the lanterns in the right direction and modifying them to achieve the required end – focus to hard or soft, gobo in, shutter or barndoor.

The lighting designer will usually stand on the ground and direct an LX team who will carry out the actual manual work – focusing the lanterns and moving ladders.

To do a good job of focusing the lighting designer must understand the following:

1) Essential Preparation before the Focus
Obviously you cannot focus a rig if you do not know what the intention of the lighting is. Remember the lighting plan will not tell you this. A plan is only a means to an efficiently installed rig. The ideas behind the design are only in the mind of the lighting designer – the reason for any lantern to be placed in any particular position and with a particular colour in it remain, for the most part, undeclared on the paper plan.

Ensure, therefore, that you know what all your equipment is there to do. This may sound obvious

Focusing.

but, in fact, with a lighting rig of any reasonable size (fifty plus units, perhaps), it is quite easy to forget what any one of them may be doing. Or worse, to mistake one for another and start by mis-focusing part of the rig and having to undo mistakes, and hence waste time and energy.

Before starting to focus, remind yourself of what the rig is supposed to be achieving. It might, after all, be several days since you have thought about it in this way. Annotate a copy of the lighting plan to aid you, if you did not do so at the time you drew it. Once again it is only too easy to think that you will remember something when it is fresh in your mind at the drafting stage.

If you are focusing someone else's rig – doing a relight – then it becomes even more essential that you have understood the intention of every unit that now surrounds you as you start the focusing session.

2) Starting the Focus

You will have to make a decision on where to start the focusing. This basically comes down to the following:

Either start where it is easiest or most convenient to – this will allow you a positive beginning and set you off at a good quick rhythm and pace, *or* start at the hardest place to get to and the hardest focuses to achieve. This will allow you to undertake the greatest challenges while you and your team are still fresh.

You may have enough people and access equipment available to allow you to have two people (or more) focusing for you at once, alternating your attention from one to the other. But do not let them set the pace. Work quickly, but not so quickly that you make a sloppy job of the focus or are rushed into bad decisions.

3) The Working Environment

Concentration is paramount during this time, and so a quiet and generally sympathetic working environment should be established. Some lighting designers like to work with music playing in the background. Some, in dead silence, some in more relaxed conversational mode.

It is usual for working lights to be switched off, and only those units that the lighting designer is addressing to be illuminated. A little ambient light may be helpful, a light on the production desk, or wherever, to help the lighting designer read the plan and write notes.

For safety reasons a total blackout should be avoided where possible during this session.

If things are not going well for other departments – the set is behind in being completed – it may be that you are asked to wait or make do.

The choice here is yours, but developing the ability to focus lanterns with working light on will save you a lot of hassle, keep you and everyone else on schedule, and generally win you friends.

Whilst focusing, take time to check your work – especially if coming back to it will involve a nightmare of moving ladders.

If other departments are invading what should be your time, they may not mind if you turn the working lights off occasionally to check an area before moving on. But remember to warn them before doing so.

4) Focusing the Intention

Have clearly in your mind what each unit is supposed to be doing. Do not be easily tempted to deviate from your course. Many things may occur to you as you focus – a unit might look particularly good doing something you had not thought of, or had another unit for – but unless you are able to think through all the repercussions of changing direction whilst 'on your feet', do not be enticed to do so or you may find yourself unable to achieve what you had hoped for.

5) The Focusing Order

Initially you may find it easier to focus lanterns in groups dictated by their use – the front cover, the gobo wash, and so on. But these units are most likely and, by necessity, not going to be all sitting right next to each other. In order to focus in groups you will have to keep moving your access equipment back and forth across the theatre space, covering the same ground again and again.

The focusing will go much more quickly if you develop the ability to go from lantern to nearest lantern, regardless of its use. If the intention of each unit, and how it belongs to a greater whole is clear in your mind, then it should not involve too much strain to chop and change in this way. The time saved will be of great benefit later.

Having said this, it is always possible to illuminate units that you have already focused to remind yourself how the one you are about to do fits into the group. Although, once again, if you do this on every occasion you will find that it will inevitably slow you down.

Have faith in your own abilities and resist the urge to check how you are doing at every turn. This is also true of the desire to start building pictures with the lighting. Use the facility to do so sparingly – only when you really have to.

6) Concentration during Focusing

Look at all aspects of the light coming from the lantern that you are focusing – not only those that you want. Check that it not only covers the area you want, for example, but also does not shine into the audience's eyes or spill onto a part of the set you would rather it did not. Look at every edge of the beam – shutter or barndoor as necessary. Check for unforeseen problems.

In the same vein, if you are not otherwise using them, close in the barndoors on a fresnel or PC to the point where they do not quite touch the beam, in order to prevent any unwanted secondary spillage or glare. This is called 'boxing in'. I have even seen profile units barndoored for the very same reason.

7) Light for Height

As focusing is carried out without performers, it is most important to remember not to focus

to the floor of the stage, but to the correct height to light the action.

In checking beams in this way, the lighting designer may have someone spare to 'walk' the stage for them. Or they may need to do so themselves. This is perfectly natural as the lighting designer will often find it easier to be on stage in order to direct the focuser anyway.

It is important that the lighting designer resists the temptation to look into the beam of light. This is a dangerous thing to do, as a habit like this will only result in damaging the lighting designer's best tool – their eyes. Also because, in the short term, it means that the lighting designer will be temporarily blinded and unable to continue at full capacity.

A better solution to the need to check the beam for position in this way is to stand in the beam with your back to the light and check its position against your shadow. Where your shadow lies in the beam makes it very clear as to how well the beam would be lighting a performer.

8) Communication during Focusing

Give clear and unequivocal directions to the person focusing for you. Left/right, up/down, left-hand shutter, right side of the beam, and so on. Use hand signals if necessary but make them clear. Do not point vaguely around. Also do not be afraid to move around the space indicating where you want the beam to begin and end, or be centred.

In order to achieve this clarity, do not be afraid to use simple terms like 'bigger' and 'smaller' – although some alternatives are just as often acceptable – 'open out' for bigger, 'close down' or 'spot it' for smaller.

The object here is, obviously, not to mystify the focuser but to get on – time is always the enemy in these sessions.

As mentioned above, it is not unusual for the lighting designer to be saying 'on me' or 'centred here' and then turn away from the beam in order not to be blinded. If you are focusing in this way make sure that, when the focus is done to your satisfaction, you move out of the beam to check it from other perspectives, thus avoiding problems you could not see whilst surrounded by light.

You need to get the job of focusing done with the minimum of fuss and as quickly as possible. At the same time, you need to balance this against the fact that you may not have time to come back to many of these units again – so you need to get it right, and maximize all your opportunities.

9) Focusing Problems
Any number of things can occur once you have come into the theatre space, and all the forward planning in the world cannot anticipate everything.

Equipment can fail and need time-consuming attention; it can fail to achieve what you hoped it would. The set may not be quite where you thought it would be; colours may not be registering as you thought they would. When problems such as these occur, keep calm and deal with them in such a way as to prevent falling too far behind. Certainly colours can be substituted, and units re-rigged or replaced but too much of this sort of thing and you will run out of time. Where quick solutions are not available it may be better to leave the problem until the rest of the rig has been attended to.

A calm appraisal of any problem is always going to be better than anything decided in panic. Although it is a good thing to be able to rethink your equipment usage on your feet, thinking through problems at a quiet time later – even overnight – can often result in a better solution being found.

A good production manager should be reasonably sympathetic to problems that you may be having that could not have been foreseen, and will help you find time and ways to resolve them.

If you are running out of time, prioritize the equipment that is most necessary to be able to proceed with the lighting session, and leave the 'luxury' equipment until a later 'catch-up' time.

Leave for later those units that are going to be doing things that a director will not feel absolutely necessary in the plotting session, and for which they can wait until the technical rehearsal or a dress rehearsal to see. But do not make promises that you cannot keep. Be rational and realistic, and be honest about what you are going to be able to achieve in any 'catch-up' session.

Also leave for later those units that will be easy to come back to later or dealt with in a spare moment – for example, equipment on the floor or low enough on a boom to be reached without access equipment.

If really desperate for time, simplify your ideas – focus only one set of top-lights for example when you know, at a pinch, you can probably manage with only one. Reduce your set dressing, and so on. If you are lucky you may have time to get back to it later, but do not bank on this, either.

PLOTTING

Having successfully focused the lighting rig, the next event on the production schedule for the

Lighting designer in rehearsals (Geoffrey Williams, Yentl).

lighting designer is the plotting session. This is the session where all the separate lighting states are created. The cues are carefully crafted to suit the moment, and time taken to ensure their place in the flow of the production.

In a small space, the creative team and lighting board operator may be sitting close together. In a bigger space, communication between lighting designer and operator may be over a headphones system (usually known as 'cans').

Plotting can happen in a number of ways, all have their strengths and weaknesses.

Pre-Plotting

The lighting designer may have time prior to a formal plotting session to prepare some or all of the lighting states. Pre-plotting has the obvious advantage of saving time later.

If this is to be the only plotting session and the director, busy elsewhere, has left the lighting designer to it, then it is as well to make sure that as much information has been gleaned from the director as possible.

However, the time may be wasted – the director may not agree with the way that the lighting designer has used the rig. Although the rig may be actually fine, a basic disagreement about the general level of light in an early cue may well mean all subsequent cues need changing in relation to it.

A better use of pre-plotting time is for the lighting designer to prepare blocks of useful units. This will certainly speed up plotting – for example, on a memory board, group together all units that are to be used together such as front cover light from one side, gobo cover, colour washes, and so on. Do not just group these units together at the same level. If the lighting control will allow it, make sure that the relative levels in a group are sympathetic to the use you will be making of them.

Rough plotting of cues in this session may also be useful, leaving the 'fine tuning' of cues for the formal plotting session.

Formal Plotting

Plotting is usually carried out in the presence of the director and the deputy stage manager. The set designer is often also present.

Each cue is built to the satisfaction of the lighting designer, director, designer and all relevant parties. The DSM puts the cueing point for the commencement of each lighting change into the script to be cued from – 'the book'.

This session can take a long time and preparation for it is essential. Pre-plotted groups of lanterns are useful as described above. The lighting designer may be happy working from the plan but may also consider making a 'crib sheet' of circuit numbers to help speed up the calling for units.

Cues can change greatly once the cast and every other element of the production is present, and so again a reasonably rough plot may be more sensible at this point.

The acting cast will not be present, and thus other persons – a number of the LX crew or an ASM for example – may be asked to 'walk' that is, stand in for the cast in areas to be lit. Having someone 'walk' can slow down things down as you often find that you spend a long time lighting them in places where the actual cast never go or only pass through fleetingly. However this is the last time that the director will be able to give their full attention to the lighting and so many will prefer to take time at this point to satisfy themselves that the lighting is as good as it can be.

Plotting During the Tech

Often it seems that the whole lighting plot changes radically once the production moves into the technical rehearsal process. Because of this, it has become quite common nowadays to plot only enough information with which to start a tech and then undertake major adjustments (or the actual plotting itself) during this session.

In such cases, the lighting designer is usually left alone to make the original plot and has to compete in the tech, amongst the many other demands, for the director's attention.

Actually the fact that there are many other elements in a tech that will stop the rehearsal, and demand attention, means that the lighting designer has time to get much done without even appearing to hold things up.

This system has the advantage of allowing the real lighting to be plotted with full stage crew, cast and apparatus and eliminates wasted time. It does not need to take more time than a formal plot would, however ...

Disadvantages with this method are that the technical rehearsal, which is a stressful time for many departments and the acting company already, becomes slower and longer.

Successful Plotting Techniques

In a formal plotting session, rough plot elements will inevitably change in the tech', such as timings; do not waste time and linger unnecessarily on things that will inevitably change later anyway. Make good use of the director whilst you have their undivided attention.

Get the feel right if not the detail. At the very least make sure you know where each cue is supposed to be and what is required of it. Get the right areas lit and in the right mood. It is sometimes easier to do this without a person 'walking' – leaving it until the tech to get the performers lit. This, after all, is usually not as difficult as getting the perfect mood, or continuity between cues.

When undertaking the initial plot *do not* set levels too high. Leave yourself somewhere to go. A good starting level is between 40 per cent and 60 per cent.

Take good notes. Make sure you write down everything that comes up from this session. Changes may be needed to any number of things and the director may be expecting to see

them efficiently done by the next session – so do not run the risk of forgetting any.

Plotting Cues

The section above describes several useful plotting techniques, but what of the actual substance of the lighting itself?

What actually happens during the plotting session is that the creative team – jointly led by lighting designer and director – build pictures. In this way we can understand lighting as being used much as Appia described it (*see* page 15) – as a bonding material between many of the diverse elements on stage, the set and the actors being the most important ones.

Each picture created from the elements on stage – not least from the elements of the lighting rig – has to have a reason to exist, a purpose and a connection with those other pictures that precede and follow.

In this manner, the creative team must weigh in the balance many factors. The lighting must not only achieve the right level of illumination, the right mood for the moment, the best means to describe the stage setting, but also make sense of the rest of the play. It must connect.

An example. A scene may need to be brightly lit, the creative team deciding that the correct atmospheric response from the lighting at this point in the play involves brightness. Having achieved this, the question should then be asked: 'Is it right that this should be the most brightly lit scene in the play?'

If not, then the lighting must leave room for another scene to be even more brightly lit – or conversely justify why this also may be as well lit.

Perhaps the other scene can be as bright but of a different, more positive hue. Perhaps the other scene is of sufficient distance away from the present cue and, following a sequence of very dark cues, may be hoped to appear even brighter in contrast. Thus the cue being presently created can afford to use the brightest rig.

Such justification must be logically found for every cue – the lighting designer should naturally already have a reason for the elements that are being provided in the rig – and thus this should not be too difficult. It simply requires that the team considers not only each cue on its own merits but also on its place in the production as a whole. Naturally very much the same applies to the placing and timing of cues.

The Technical Rehearsal

This, often long, session, always incorporates many stops and starts as all the technical elements are slotted into place, rehearsed and re-rehearsed over and over. It is a time for the lighting designer to see cues run and states acted in. The lighting designer can make adjustments to the timings and placing of cues as well as to the content of the cues themselves.

Much replotting can get done whilst the session has stopped for other reasons and, as such, a lighting designer should develop the ability to work fast and use such moments.

Obviously it is ideal if nothing goes wrong or needs adjusting in this session. But this rarely happens. The lighting designer is allowed to stop things themselves if they need to – maybe to rerun a cue or make any kind of adjustment. However the session will only tolerate so many occasions without it becoming obvious that time will run out, so use your time judiciously – only interrupt things if you feel you cannot make an adjustment later.

Otherwise, keep very attentive. Do not miss seeing cues happen by making notes, 'nose in book', but nevertheless do note all the things that need adjusting and get back to them as soon as you have a chance.

Remember, on a modern lighting board an amazing amount of fine tuning can be done quickly and efficiently in a very short space of time.

Technical Work

After the technical rehearsal, and every other such session, there may be time allocated for 'technical work on stage'. This is time when any of the technical departments, or all together, may use the stage to make changes or finish off work.

The lighting designer, like everyone else, needs to negotiate the use of the space with whomever is in charge, usually the production manager or stage manager.

Other rehearsal sessions will inevitably give rise to further notes and there may well be other 'technical work' sessions booked further ahead in the schedule. Thus, there is no point in going to an inaccessible part of the rig if it is just as likely that you may need to return to it again. So it makes perfect sense to leave some (but not too many) of the less glaringly important things to do later.

It is important to use this time well and therefore to prioritize the things you need to do sensibly. Do as much as you can under working lights before requesting 'dark time' on stage.

Sharing the stage during this session is one thing, getting 'dark time' to replot cues or refocus may be more difficult. This will need to be

Director Nona Shepphard taking notes in the technical rehearsal.

separately negotiated. Often it is possible to take a different break from everyone else and thus have the stage whilst everyone else is away.

Generally, as with most things, the trick is to work fast but efficiently, and to use your time well.

Dress Rehearsals

Much the same applies to dress rehearsals as to watching a run. Be ready in good time and remember that you may need to arrange a torch or low-level light to be able to see what you are writing.

The lighting designer must be prepared to take quick and coherent notes, to keep their eye on the stage and not on the page. For this reason it is a good idea to develop a shorthand – for example:

$$Q6 \quad C4, 7, 10 \uparrow 15$$

which translates as:

in cue 6 channels 4, 7, 10, need to go up by 15 per cent.

If you are using such a shorthand, draw a line under each note or number them in order so that each is clearly separated from the other.

Monitoring and the DSM

Good use of the monitoring and communication equipment will save a lot of time later.

If the theatre is using a 'cans' system then it is very useful to be able to communicate with the lighting board operator during this session. It is generally considered OK to replot during the action so long as the operator is not on standby for the next cue.

Even when a show is generally too busy to allow for much replotting it is still useful to be able to hear the DSM call the cues. It tells the lighting designer if the cues are being correctly called and, if so, whether the timing or placing of a cue needs adjusting.

The use of a separate monitor displaying the lighting board's output information allows the lighting designer to compare the cues running on stage with what the board is actually doing. It specifically allows the lighting designer to check the content of a cue down to the separate levels of each channel.

Notes Sessions

Notes sessions follow dress rehearsals. The director takes the lead on these occasions and will usually hold separate acting and technical note sessions.

Be attentive, have your paperwork with you so that you can answer enquiries like:

'What is the timing on cue 6?'
'What did we think of cue 15?'
'Where is cue 7 given?';

As with the latter case, you may need assistance from the DSM to answer; they, too, should have the information at their fingertips and be fully informed.

If you have notes that you also want to give, it is acceptable to take over the session after the director – or if they all concern the DSM, perhaps seek a 'one-to-one' session afterwards. Use the general notes session for things that need discussing in a wider group, or that you want the director to specifically hear.

Opening Night and after

In an ideal world the final dress rehearsal should represent the final product, and this is certainly something to be aiming for. However, usually there are still a few notes given even after the rehearsal.

Hopefully, by this point you should only be dealing with the niceties of adding half a point to a unit in one cue, or nudging the focus of a unit up-stage a little, and so on. But this will, of course, still take time.

Indeed, it may be necessary to return after the opening night to rectify any faults that still seem apparent. If the production is 'running' for a long period it may also make sense to come back and check that the rig, and thus the lighting, has not deteriorated over time through neglect.

The lighting designer, along with the other members of the creative team, should always be looking for improvement. Because of this, it is likely that they will always have notes, even after the first night. However, the time must come when you need to move on to new challenges. You have to acquire an ability to see that what you have achieved is of a standard more than high enough, and that you can thus 'let the piece go'.

Whatever the case, the first night can be a time of great nerves even though, or especially because, all the lighting designer can do at this point is sit back and enjoy. And it is certainly worth trying to cultivate the ability to relish this moment – when all the hard work finally comes to fruition.

CONCLUSION

The focus and plot are integral components of the lighting process.

Chapter 13 includes a number of photographs of lighting of various degrees of accomplishment. As part of this, alongside the placing of equipment and other factors, the focus, in particular, can be seen here to be a crucial factor in their success.

Circumstances and individuals change drastically from production to production. Ideally then, the lighting designer should be able to work both roughly and quickly, or painstakingly and over a lengthy time period, reacting to each new team and circumstance and be able to take full advantage of the situation that is presented, or dictated by others.

The ability to blend your working methods in with your particular team will save a great deal of heartache – and could be said to be every bit as important as the ability to get the right mood for the production itself.

Focusing and plotting are the very essence of the art of successful lighting design.

13 THE ART OF LIGHTING

INTRODUCTION

Let us now summarize all that has been discussed in this book with some examples of real lighting designs – good and bad.

These illustrations, culled from the Rada archive, serve to highlight many of the other things that have been discussed in this book.

The first two, although not photos of the best quality, nevertheless show only too clearly what appears to be bad focusing. On what they are, when and by whom, I shall remain generally silent. Indeed I sincerely apologize to anyone involved – I am sure the photos are just unfortunate and do not represent the true quality of work involved. Nevertheless, they do help us here.

Let us begin with the *Wood Demon*. The general feel of the lighting here is really not at all bad. Note how, by design or focus, one is only too aware of the light through doorways and onto certain pieces of furniture. A good general cover should look as if it is part of the set – that it belongs to the space – not just appears to serve the action.

Also note how the practical light, up-stage centre, only serves to light a small area around it and little else – surely this could have been better used to suggest a main source of light for the scene. Indeed, it could have been used to justify a strong beam of light around the adjacent doorway at least.

Next, we turn to *Saved* (*see* overleaf). Although this scene has a 'washed-out' look appropriate for the bleak hospital of its setting, once again the separate beams of light that make up the 'cover' are only too apparent on the set walls.

The Wood Demon,
Anton Chekov.

Saved, *Edward Bond.*

Measure for Measure,
William Shakespeare.

Also bad focusing (or perhaps the scenery has been badly set) has resulted in a very ugly shadow coming across the back wall and door.

Additionally, the practical light fitting seems too distant from the scene for it to be playing any part in the lighting here.

The photograph on the right shows a more successful blending of set and action. The free-standing unit in the background depicts bright sunlight coming, at an angle, into the room. The heroine in the foreground, although inevitably lit from 'out front', nevertheless shows a single strong shadow only (on her shoulder) that would not be out of keeping with this. Her face, though, is more than visible but, like her costume, interestingly highlighted.

With regard to *Death of a Salesman*, set designers please note – if the set is to be acted upon, and therefore lit, a white object amongst otherwise subdued colours is likely to radiate. But then perhaps one could say that the refrigerator is central to the American provincial life as depicted in this play!

Lighting designers can ask for such items to be 'broken down' – that is, dulled. Similarly mirrors can be sprayed down. But obviously if the thing is supposed to look pristine there is a limit to what can be done.

The scene from *The Caretaker* looks perfect for the dull and grubby world of the play, and we can just believe the practical is supplying the pool of light below. However the light level is not high and it may be necessary to subtly lift it once the action of the play has begun.

Death of a Salesman,
Arthur Miller.

BELOW: **The Caretaker,**
Harold Pinter.

Dona Rosita, the Spinster,
F.G. Lorca.

The lighting in the scene from *Dona Rosita the Spinster* also looks apt. But this is the 'preset' – lighting for when the audience enters the theatre. The light apparently coming through the window is, in fact, being projected by a gobo from in front, rather than from behind, the set, which is due to the lack of space behind the set.

The lights will go down to announce the beginning of the play, and when they reappear the window will not seem to be producing the same light, as this cheat will be only too obviously revealed by the action

Next, from *A Month in the Country*, is a beautiful photograph of lighting that meets nearly all requirements. It looks right, it sets a sunny mood beautifully, it will sufficiently light the action, and it sets off the set well.

In fact, only the faintest of shadows outside the window and on the floor give away the fact that this is not a real country house in midsummer, but a lighting state made from any number of lanterns.

Finally, from *Birds on the Wing*, an example that takes us through the complete process. This musical had its world premiere at the Westminster Theatre in London in the spring of 2000. It was written and directed by Guy Slater, with songs and lyrics by Ken Howard and Alan Blaikley. The set and costumes were designed by Matthew Wright, and it was lit by the author. *Birds on the Wing* took for its inspiration Aristophanes's play *Lysistrata*, updating it to the London of the late 1950s/early 1960s – the world of early 'rock-and-roll'. Although inevitably larger in scale than a non-musical, the piece was in some ways quite simple – with only three settings (*see* diagram opposite).

A Month in the Country, *Ivan Turgenev.*

ABOVE: **Birds on the Wing,** *Guy Slater.*

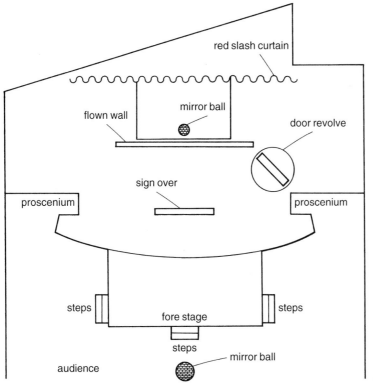

red slash curtain

flown wall

mirror ball

door revolve

sign over

proscenium

proscenium

steps

steps

fore stage

steps

audience

mirror ball

Diagram of set elements for Birds on the Wing.

* A dance hall – the full stage area, with a raised rostrum set up-stage. The Westminster's stage was built out into the auditorium, the first few rows of seating being removed. The side boxes of the theatre were used as part of the 'dance hall' setting, and the action allowed to spill onto the auditorium floor.
* Outside the dance hall, a brick wall piece is flown in, painted with appropriate graffiti.
* A company boardroom. Three large portraits of board members flown into position in front of the wall, hiding the graffiti.

There was not an enormous budget. Indeed most money went on sound amplification rather than on the set or lighting. Costumes were also quite costly as there was a cast of over twenty. The final lighting rig consisted of a mixture of equipment hired, already at the Westminster Theatre, and borrowed.

This is how the 'needs list' came to look after discussions with the director and designer, after listening to the preview tapes, and after seeing one and a half 'stagger-through' rehearsals.

* General cover for dance hall – glitzy night-time.
* General cover for dance hall – working light/daytime.
* General cover for dance hall exterior – day.
* General cover for dance hall exterior – night.
* General cover for boardroom.
* Dressing for set pieces as above.
* Lighting for musical number/dances. Specifically to make a distinction between the boys and the girls. Also between the two rival gangs.
* Follow-spot for musical numbers.
* Two mirror balls.
* Dance hall sign – practical.
* On-stage band to light.
* Rope-lights and fairy lights to be placed around the set.

Due to restrictions of time and budget, and in accordance with the nature of the piece, several decisions were made that helped things along – namely the reliance on follow-spots to light the singers – a more than acceptable device for a musical in any case.

The budget did allow for some 'intelligent lights' and scrollers, which meant that specials and colour washes could be flexible and not involve too many other units.

The 'intelligent' units were Martin MAC 500s and 600s. The former profile in nature, the latter for fresnel (or wash).

The final hand-drawn lighting design is reproduced on page 145.

The following notes refer to the needs list above and the unit circuit numbers on the plan.

GENERAL COVER (DANCE HALL – BOARDROOM) FRONT

The Westminster Theatre has very limited front-of-house positions. As such the front cover – the units that would be lighting faces – had to be positioned on the ladder section to the left and right of the circle front. Two sets of instruments were used (as available), both zoom profiles Cantata 11/26 and SL 15/32. Units 1–6 on one side, 73–78 on the other.

The central position is very high in the dome of the ceiling and presented too high an angle for most of the stage. Units 9 and 12 were to light off the front set to each side.

Up-stage cover was provided from the proscenium bar by 1k fresnel units: numbers 21, 22, 23 on one side, 96, 95, 94 on the other.

The front part of the general cover was coloured in warm colours to suit all settings and be a reasonably rich mix suitable for a lively, up-tempo, musical. Lee 152 = Pale Gold, 765 = Lee Yellow.

A dark blue colour wash (Rosco *79) was provided for the night-time scenes, using 2k PC units, numbers 8, 79, 33 and 101.

The lighting design for
Birds on the Wing.

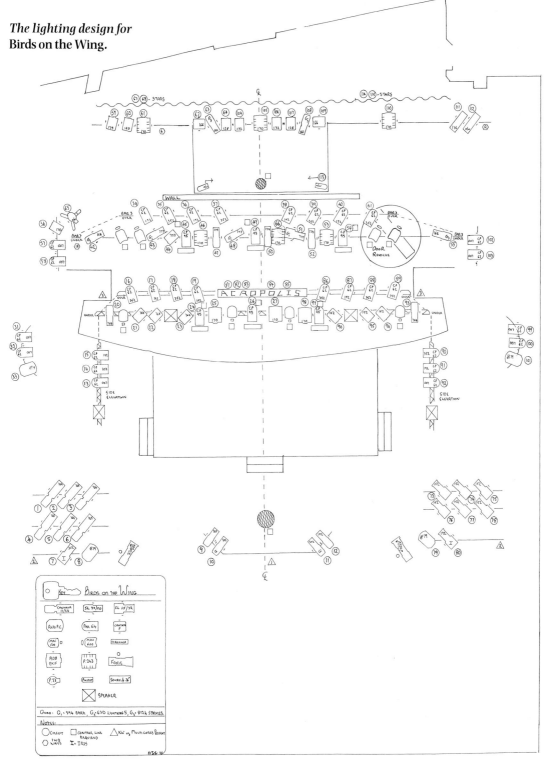

Back-Light

Back-light for most of the set was provided by the Parcans with scrollers. Units 45, 49, 54, 24, 26 and 97. In order to get the required spread they were fitted with CP 95 par bulbs – very wide beam.

The scrollers allowed the colour to be changed for different settings. The scrollers were hired with Rosco colours already made up as follows:

00 = Clear. Used as part of the daytime working light state

06 = No colour Straw. Useful when used to support general cover.

05 = Rose Tint. Used to highlight girls' and romantic songs.

371 = Theatre Booster 1 (medium blue). Used to highlight boys' songs.

79 = Bright Blue. Used to suggest night-time.

26 = Light Red. Used to highlight ribald, passionate songs.

20 = Medium Amber. Used to suggest daylight/sunshine.

339 = Broadway Pink. Also used for girls' songs.

389 = Chroma Green. Used as top light for boardroom scenes.

To facilitate transitions between musical numbers and scenes, it was necessary to provide other back/top-light, and for this to go further up-stage than the units with scrollers.

General back-light was provided by units coloured with Lee 170 = Deep Lavender. Units 61, 105, 110, 46, 66, 53, 25, 27 and 98.

Side-Light

In keeping with the musical/dance aspect of the production and to avoid overusing the otherwise rather boring front cover, a certain amount of cross- and side-light was installed, using parcans in Lee 007 (Pale Yellow) from both sides. Units 31, 32, 57, 58, 102, 103, 99 and 100.

Set Dressing

In order to highlight, and make a distinction between the settings, the set was dressed as follows:

DANCE HALL

Units on the small stage to add glitz – in Pale Red (Lee 166) units 62 and 109.

Footlights on small stage – Par 36 Beam-lights – units 113, which also lit the small mirror ball.

Gobo stars on small stage in Lee 061 (Mist Blue), Units 63 and 108.

Break up gobos across stage curtain pelmet – Lee 166 again, units 42 and 55.

Stars made from fairy lights sandwiched between backcloth and gauze – units 67, 68, 114 and 115. Separate circuits to allow for twinkling.

Backing light for the door into Hall was provided by unit 112 in open white.

The main mirror ball was often lit as part of the dance hall but only rotated during certain dance numbers – units 7 and 80 fitted with irises provided the light in colours Lee 352 (Glacier Blue) and Lee 192 (Flesh Pink).

EXTERIOR

Wall piece dressed with goboed profiles in Lee 777 (Rust) – units 43, 48, with exterior door to match – unit 51.

Lamp post given a pool of light around it from unit 44 also in Lee 777.

Backing light for the door out of the dance hall was provided by unit 111 in Lee 176 (Loving Amber).

BOARDROOM

The three pictures were lit with units 47, 50 and 52 in Lee 174 (Dark Steel Blue).

Backing light for the door into the boardroom was also provided by unit 112 in open white.

MUSICAL NUMBER/DANCES

In addition to those units already described as supporting the musical numbers, a large (in comparison to the rest of the rig) rig of parcans was provided in boy and girl colours (as on mirror ball), Lee 352 (Glacier Blue) and Lee 192 (Flesh Pink).

These units were carefully positioned to provide both vivid back- or side-lighting, and to look good to the audience. On a number of occasions the units chased in various patterns. Unit numbers: 13 to 19, 86 to 89, 34 to 41.

These units were also supported on the small stage by units 64, 104, 106 and 107 in slightly darker blues and pinks.

The MAC 600 units also provided colour washes, movement and chasing, as well as strobing during one aggressive musical number.

The MAC 500 units provided all the above plus the ability to add gobos to scenes in a subtle manner, and also in a less subtle manner during musical numbers. They were particularly good at giving the period feeling: spinning globes in a manner not unlike the 'Austin Powers' movies.

Follow-Spots

These were Robert Juliat discharge (HMI) units called 'Foxies', and held a range of colours available in their semaphore colour changers (*see* plan on page 145).

Mirror Balls

Lit as described above, the large unit in the auditorium was a 36in beast that was meant to bring the dance hall into the audience, the smaller one (a mere 12in) was meant to echo it on stage.

Dance Hall Sign

This was supported above the proscenium lighting bar and carried the name of the dance hall (Acropolis). Each letter was lit with small bulbs and allocated circuits in groups of three so that it could chase – numbers 81 to 83. The sign was also framed by a ring of other small bulbs (84) and contained an ultra-violet light to be used in the night scenes (85).

On-Stage Band

Units 59, 60, 65 and 56 lit the on-stage band – up-stage right.

Rope-Lights and Fairy Lights

In the way of all things, the designer decided he did not like these and so they were cut!

OTHER UNITS

Units 20 and 93 on the proscenium bar supported the MACs in lighting the cast who walked through the auditorium at the end of Act 1.

Units 10 and 11 in the dome were fitted with lightning gobos for a particular moment in a song.

BIRDS ON THE WING SUMMARY

I hope that by studying these notes you can begin to visualize how this production looked. You should be able to tell the richness of the colouring used and the inclusion of other rather bold elements. You should at least be able to tell what fun it was meant to be!

Also it should be clear that even for quite a big venture the ingredients were relatively simple – even when the end result needs to look quite complicated.

CONCLUSION

Photographs always lie. Certainly in the context of theatre lighting, a photographer can catch moments that, in passing, no audience can ever hope to see. Nevertheless, they can also instruct – which I hope has been the case on this occasion. Analysing our work, and that of others, can only help in the progress of our own, often hard-won, skills.

14 A Career in Lighting Design

There is no prescribed route into the theatre world, although increasingly a formal training is thought to be imperative.

Few practitioners ever believe that anything replaces training 'on the job' – which used to be the only way into such a career. However, it is increasingly difficult to get that 'job' without some preparation. Today there are a broad range of available courses at many levels.

Training

A prospective student should decide whether they want a vocational or an academic training, and look for the course that best suits them.

In order to chase an ever-decreasing pool of available grant money, many theatre schools spent the 1990s changing their once purely vocational courses to qualify for degree status. Correspondingly, many more academic courses also attempted to attract students by developing their vocational strengths.

This may be all well and good, but a student wanting to follow a career in lighting design must be careful to check that in making this transition the schools have maintained (or added) a good level of practical 'hands on' experience to their courses. Some schools added academic study (often in a plethora of only vaguely appropriate areas), and increased the length of the course to do so. They also expanded the number of students that they took. For these reasons the practical experience decreased.

The status of a degree in lighting design has yet to be really established in the 'marketplace'. More importance is often placed on electrical qualifications, for example the City and Guilds 1810 course. Several vocational courses offer these qualifications as part of theirs, or they can be taken separately as part- or full-time courses.

As a rough guide, the prospective student should check the following:

* The amount of practical work available – in class and in theatre.
* The number of productions you will work on, and in what role.
* The quality of materials – broad rage of current equipment in good theatre and studio spaces.
* The range of the course – look for CAD, intelligent lighting training as well as thorough tuition in lighting design.
* The staff/student ratio – what support will you have in your work?
* The quality of staff used – where have they worked and where were they trained, including guest lecturers?
* The opportunity for lighting design – how many productions and on what scale?
* The philosophy behind the course – how do they 'teach' lighting design, for example?

Lighting design students Sebastian Barraclough and David Bishop stand in their own creation Fanfare (Rada)*.*

* The opportunity for work experience/placement. Seek examples.
* Career prospects – what have past students gone on to do?
* Value for money – length of course versus outcomes/prospects.

TYPES OF LIGHTING DESIGNER

There are many ways to be a lighting designer. You can seek to specialize in a particular type of work – opera, dance, rock-and-roll, trade show. You can also work in theatre education. Certainly you can work as a lighting designer in a number of guises.

It is possible to work your way up through a lighting department, perhaps starting as an assistant electrician, getting as much experience of designing as possible along the way.

A theatre lighting department can have any number of employees, but there are three basic roles: Assistant Electrician, Deputy Chief

Electrician and Chief Electrician, the latter often nowadays called Head of Lighting. In a good producing company there may be opportunities to light productions for all members of the team, but more often the Head of the Department will be called upon to express such skills.

CHIEF ELECTRICIAN AS LIGHTING DESIGNER

Although not always respected as such, many a Chief LX is capable of good stage lighting. A freelance career has its minus points as well as its pluses (*see* below). For a stable and secure career, this position in a resident company suits many. Of course there is nothing to stop the Chief LX also seeking freelance work when they can.

THE FREELANCE LIGHTING DESIGNER

Lighting design does not pay particularly well – certainly not compared to the equivalent worlds of television or film, and thus a freelance career can be rather precarious. There is really only so much freelance work available, and thus only so many people can operate purely in this way at any one time. Those wishing to sacrifice some basic comforts to get a full career in this way are most likely to succeed.

Not only can the work be rather precarious, it can also be rather lonely. Working in a resident company certainly has much more of the home comforts of a 'regular' job. The need to 'network', and to be able to go as a virtual stranger from theatre to theatre will only suit a certain kind of person.

One way in which to develop one's own skills is to take on the job of relighting a production.

RELIGHTS

The need for relighting occurs when a production is moved from one theatre to another or is remounted in the original theatre – the latter possibly in a repertory situation.

Although quite a difficult job – often every bit as hard as putting the original lighting in – the job of relighting a production is often given to the company, production or stage manager who, in my experience, rarely do it as well as they might! However where a piece needs some stage electrics personnel it can also be given to them.

Relighting involves getting a good understanding of the original design concept of the production, and developing an understanding of how the original lighting design addressed the piece. It often involves having the knowledge to replace the original equipment with what is available in a new space – as well as adapting the design to fit a different-shaped auditorium.

As a relight often has to be undertaken in limited time and against a general routine of organized chaos, it is vital that you have good paperwork to work from and have undertaken to discuss the lighting with the original lighting designer and/or designer in some depth. Or, better still, had the opportunity to watch the original process unfold.

TOURING

The job of touring can be arduous and challenging. If the lighting designer is touring with a production it is unlikely that they will have an easy time of things. Venues can be underequipped and understaffed. The resident electrics staff, who work on production after production, and who have no relation to your production anyway, are usually not interested in the creative part of the work at all, and simply want to get to the bar as soon as possible!

Also as the production will make more money if it plays for longer in each venue, it is not uncommon to have to open a show on the same day as the get in. Again, good paperwork and a clear mind are essential.

Lighting for Touring

It is possible to design the lighting of the original show to suit touring, keeping it simple, unfussy and yet effective. The simpler it is, the more time will be available to make it look good in each venue.

Whereas, in a resident situation, you may design with units that are expected to do several jobs – perhaps as part of a general cover – for touring this can lead to serious problems, as each venue makes you compromise one role of the unit for another. If you keep the use of each unit in your rig clear this will make it easier to accommodate each new situation. Also it will be especially helpful to someone who is going to have to relight the production.

To help a relight situation it is a good idea to create clear notes of what each unit is supposed to achieve. Or even, if possible, draw a new design for each venue, or write some rough guidelines.

The Nature of the Work

Theatre work involves long and unsocial hours. A production week can involve day after day of fourteen hours or more. Work on productions and trade shows can involve toiling through the night and over weekends. As I have said above it does not pay particularly well although it can be vastly rewarding.

The work can instill a great group feeling, and labouring amongst those who work in the industry can be enormous fun. It is a vocation as much as it is a job and, as such, will only suit some. In many ways there is much to be said for dabbling in it at an 'amateur' level, and no reason why the finished product should be any the less for that.

Networking

A freelance lighting designer will get work if they prove to be skilled and speedy at what they do – the first produces excellence, the second saves money. But a part of this process is also the ability to deal well with the necessary people – usually directors and designers. If standing in the bar between acts or after the show making small talk is an anathema to you, you are perhaps less likely to succeed.

Having an Agent

Having stated that lighting designers are underpaid, it may go against the grain to give a percentage of your meagre earnings to an agent. Indeed some lighting designers manage well enough without them. The same can perhaps also be said of accountants.

An agent does save the lighting designer from having to deal with fees or royalties, and leaves them free just to turn up and do the job.

Actors nearly always have agents and some of these handle designers and directors also. An agent may specialize in the technical and creative team members, or you may find that you are the only lighting designer on their books. After all, the industry cannot support that many freelance lighting designers.

You would expect an agent to have good enough contacts to be able to put your name forward from time to time to other of their clients, or suggest you if another of their clients is unavailable. However, agents seldom actually get you jobs.

Conclusion

The job of lighting designer is one that I have found to be extremely rewarding. The combination of the technical and the artistic seems to strike a chord with me that I cannot really describe or define. I hope this book will inspire some others to take this route and, hopefully, make their way that bit easier.

To everyone tinkering in the realm of light I wish the brightest of futures.

NOTES

I am particularly indebted to two invaluable reference books for pointing me in the right direction when researching Chapters 1 and 8. I would recommend them highly – they are:

Nagler, A.M., *A Source Book in Theatrical History* (Dover Publications, Inc., New York, 1952).

Carlson, Marvin, *Theories of the Theatre* (Cornell University Press, Ithaca and London, 1984). Expanded edition, 1993.

See also Further Reading on page 155.

Chapter 1: A Lighting History

1. Craig, Edward Gordon *Books and Theatres.*
2. Pollux: 'Extracts concerning the Greek theatre and masks' in *Aristotle's Poetics; or discourses concerning tragic and epic imitation* (London, 1775).
3. Nagler, A.M., op. cit., p. 41.
4. Vasari, Giorgio *The Lives of the Painters, Sculptors and Architects*, trans. A.B. Hinds (New York: E.P. Dutton & Co., 1927).
5. Pilbrow, Richard *Stage Lighting Design. The Art, the Craft, the Life* (Nick Hern Books, London, 1997).
6. Serlio, Sebastiano *The First Book of Architecture* (London, 1611).
7. Ibid.
8. Di Somi, Leon Ebreo *Dialoghi* (MS Biblioteca Palatina, Parma). Trans. Salvatore J. Castiglione. *See* Nagler, p. 102.
9. Sabbattini, Nicola *Practica di fabrica scene e machine ne teatri* (Ravenna, 1638).
10. Hertford, Charles H. and Simpson, Percy (eds) *Ben Jonson* (Oxford: The Clarendon Press, 1925–47)
11. Chappuzeau, Samuel *Le Théâtre Français* (1674, reprinted Brussels, 1867).
12. Ménestrier, C.F. *Des représentations en musique anciennes et modernes* (Paris, 1684).
13. Algarotti, Francesco *Saggio l'opera in Musica* (1755).
14. Nagler, op cit., p. 311.
15. Wickham, Glyn *A History of the Theatre* (Phaidon Press, London, 1985), p. 181.
16. Rees, Terence *Theatre Lighting in the Age of Gas* (The Society for Theatre Research, 1978), p. 52.
17. Ibid., p. 72
18. Pilbrow, Richard op. cit., p. 174.
19. Pilbrow, Richard op. cit., p. 175
20. Brook, Peter *Threads of Time – a Memoir* (Methuen Drama, 1999), p. 48.
21. Strindberg, A. *Miss Julie.* Preface, trans Edwin Bjørkman (Charles Scribner's Sons, New York, 1912).
22. Appia, Adolphe *La mise en scène du drama Wagnérian* (Paris, 1895).
23. Appia, Adolphe *Die Musik und die Inscenierung* (Munich, 1899).
24. Carlson, Marvin op cit., p. 293.
25. Selden, Samuel and Sellman, Hunton, D. *Stage Scenery and Lighting – a Handbook for Non-Professionals* (George G. Harrap & Co. Ltd, 1930), p. 207.

26. Selden, Samuel and Sellman, Hunton D. op. cit., p. 210.
27. Goffin, Peter *Stage Lighting for Amateurs* (Frederick Muller Ltd, London, 1938), p. 80.
28. Fuchs, George *Revolution in the Theatre*, trans. Constance Kuhn (Ithaca, 1959), p. 85.
29. Craig, E.G. *On the Art of the Theatre* (Heinemann, London, 1911), p. 22.
30. Ibid., p. 41.
31. Ibid., p. 163.
32. Ibid., p. 164.
33. Goffin, op. cit., p. 85.
34. Symons, Arthur *Plays, Acting and Music* (New York, 1909), p. 165.
35. Segel, Harold *Twentieth Century Russian Drama* (New York, 1979), p. 65.
36. Komissarzhevsky, Fyodor *Myself and the Theatre* (New York, 1920), p. 71.
37. Ibid., p. 149.
38. Marinetti, F. *La volupté d'être sifflé* (new York, 1972), p. 113.
39. Prampolini, Enrico 'Futuristic Scenography', trans. V.N. Kirby in *Futuristic Performance* (New York, 1971), p. 204.
40. Depero, Fortunato *Il teatro plastico* (Luglio, 1970), pp. 147–8.
41. Tzara, Tristan 'Le dadaisme et la théâtre', in *Oeuvres complètes* (Paris, 1975). Vol. 1 p. 564.
42. Witkiewicz, Stanislaw *The Madman and the Nun and Other Plays*, trans. Daniel C. Gerould and C.S. Durer (Seattle, 1968), pp. 292–3.
43. Styan, J.L. *Modern Drama in Theory and Practice: 3 – Expressionism and Epic Theatre* (Cambridge University Press, 1981).
44. Ritchie, J.M. *The Scene is Changed* (Berlin, 1919) p. 52
45. Carter, Huntley *The Theatre of Max Reinhardt* (1914) pp. 232–3.
46. Carlson, Marvin op. cit., p. 352.
47. Gropius, Walter 'Der Arbeit der Bauhausbühne' from *Die Bauhausbühne, Erste Mittelung* (Weimar, 1922).
48. Schreyer, Lothar 'Das Bühnenwerk' from *Bauhausbühne, Erste Mittelung* (Weimar, 1922).
49. Belasco, D. *Theatre through its Stage Door* Harper & Brothers (New York, 1919).
50. MacGowan, Kenneth 'The New Path of the Theatre', *Theatre Arts 3* (1919), p. 88.
51. Baty, Gaston *Rideau baissé* (Paris, 1949), p. 219.
52. Brecht, B. 'Über experimentelles Theater' from *Theater der Zeit* (East Berlin, 1959).
53. Brecht, B. *Antigonemodell* (West Berlin, 1949).
54. Brecht, B. *Couragemodell* (East Berlin, 1958).
55. Styan, op. cit., p. 143.
56. Brecht, B. 'Der Bühnenbau des epischen Theaters' quoted *from Brecht on Theatre – the development of an Aesthetic* ed. and trans. by John Willets (Methuen, 1957), p. 141.
57. Esslin, M. *The Theatre of the Absurd* trans. C. Richards (Grove Press, New York, 1958).
58. Grotowski, Jerzy *Towards a Poor Theatre* (New York, 1968), p. 21.
59. Peter Brook *The Shifting Point – Forty Years of Theatrical Exploration 1946–1987* (Methuen Drama, 1987), p. 14.

Chapter 8: Modern Lighting Theory

1. Pilbrow, Richard *Stage Lighting* (Nick Hern Books, London, 1970), p. 18.
2. Ost, Geoffrey *Stage Lighting* (Herbert Jenkins, London).
3. McCandless, Stanley *A Method of Lighting the Stage* (Theatre Arts Books, New York, 1932).
4. Luckiesh, M. *The Lighting Art* (D. Van Nostrand and Co., New York, 1916).
5. Ridge, C. Harold *Stage Lighting for 'Little' Theatres* (W. Heffer & Sons Ltd., Cambridge, 1925).

6. Hartman, Louis *Theatre Lighting* (d. Appleton, New York, 1930).

7. Selden S., and Sellman, H.D. *Stage Scenery and Lighting* (George G. Harrap & Co. Ltd., London, 1930), pp. 384–5.

8. Fuchs, Theodore *Stage Lighting* (Little Brown & Co., Boston, 1929).

9. Ridge, C. Harold op. cit., pp. 5–7.

10. Ibid., pp. 12–18.

11. Ibid., p. 72

12. Ibid., pp. 73–4.

13. Ibid., p. 77.

14. McCandless, Stanley op. cit. Foreword to the fourth edition – 1958, p. 7.

15. Ibid., pp. 8 and 9.

16. Ibid., p. 14.

17. Ibid., pp. 18–19.

18. Ibid., pp. 50, 51.

19. Ibid., p. 53.

20. Ibid., pp. 55, 56.

21. Ibid., p. 79.

22. Goffin, Peter *Stage Lighting for Amateurs* (Frederick Muller Ltd, London 1938) p. 79.

23. Ibid., p. 74.

24. Ost, Geoffrey op. cit., pp. 13 and 34.

25. Bentham, Frederick *Stage Lighting* (Pitman & Sons, London, 1950).

26. Gayford, Martin, Arts Review, *Daily Telegraph*, 8/5/01.

27. Pilbrow, Richard op. cit., p. 12.

28. Ibid., pp. 14–16.

29. Reid, Francis *The Stage Lighting Handbook* (A. & C. Black, London, 1976).

30. Streader, T. and Williams, J. *Create Your Own Stage Lighting* (Bell & Hyman, 1985).

31. Morgan, Nigel H. *Stage Lighting for Designers* (Herbert Press, 1995).

32. Fraser, Neil *Lighting and Sound* (Phaidon Press, 1988).

33. Fraser, Neil *Stage Lighting Design: a Practical Guide* (The Crowood Press, 1999).

FURTHER READING

Beginner's Guide to Theatre Lighting

Fraser, Neil, *Lighting and Sound*, 2nd ed. (Phaidon Press, 1991).

Fraser, Neil, *Stage Lighting Design* (The Crowood Press, 1999).

Morgan, Nigel H., *Stage Lighting for Theatre Designers* (Herbert Press, 1995).

Reid, Francis, *The ABC of Stage Lighting* (A. & C. Black, 1992).

The Stage Lighting Handbook, 5th ed. (A. & C. Black, 1996).

Streader, T. and J. Williams, *Create Your Own Stage Lighting* (Bell & Hyman, 1985).

Advanced Guides to Theatre Lighting

Bentham, Frederick, *The At of Stage Lighting* (Pitman House, 1980).

Fraser, Neil, *Stage Lighting Design: a Practical Guide* (The Crowood Press, 1999).

Pilbrow, Richard, *Stage Lighting Design – the Art, the Craft, the Life* (Nick Hern Books, 1997).

Reid, Francis, *Discovering Stage Lighting* (Focal Press, 1993).

Reid, Francis, *Lighting the Stage* (Focal Press, 1995).

Walne, Graham (ed.), *Effects for the Theatre* (A. & C. Black, 1995).

Projection for the Performing Arts (Focal Press).

Theatre Theory and its History

Artaud, A., *The Theatre and Its Double* (Calder Publications, 1970).

Brecht on Theatre – the Development of an Aesthetic, (ed. and transl.) John Willett (Methuen Drama, 1964).

Bentley, Eric (ed.) *The Theory of the Modern Stage* (Penguin Books, 1968).

Brandt, George W. (ed.) *Modern Theories of Drama* (Clarendon Press, Oxford, 1998)

Brook, Peter, *The Shifting Point – Forty Years of Theatrical Exploration 1946–1987* (Methuen Drama, 1987).

Brook, Peter, *The Open Space* (Penguin, 1970).

Brook, Peter, *Threads of Time – a Memoir* (Methuen Drama, 1999).

Carlson, Marvin, *Theories of the Theatre* (Cornell University Press, 1984 – expanded edition 1993).

Condron, Frances, Michael Fraser and Stuart Sutherland, *Guide to Digital Resources for the Humanities* (CTI Centre for Textual Studies, Humanities Computing Unit, University of Oxford, 2000).

Esslin, Martin, *The Theatre of the Absurd* (Penguin Books, revised 1968).

Gaskill, William, *A Sense of Direction* (Faber & Faber, 1988).

Grotowski, Jerzy, *Towards a Poor Theatre* (Methuen, 1968).

Innes, Christopher, *Modern British Drama 1890–1990* (Cambridge University Press, 1992).

Innes, Christopher, *Avant Garde Theatre 1892–1992* (Routledge, Inc., NY, 1993).

Nagler, A.M., *A Source Book in Theatrical History* (Dover Publications, Inc., NY, 1952).

Rees, Terence, *Theatre Lighting in the Age of Gas* (The Society for Theatre Research, 1978).

Styan, J.L. *Modern Drama in Theory and Practice* (Vols 1–3) (Cambridge University Press, 1981).

Wickham, Glyn, *A History of the Theatre* (Phaidon Press, 1985).

USEFUL WEBSITES

Organizations

ABTT – Association of British Theatre
Technicians
http://www.abtt.org.uk

ALD – Association of Lighting Designers
http://www.ald.org.uk/

BECTU – Broadcast Entertainment
Cinematograph & Theatre Union
http://www.bectu.org.uk

Entertainment Technology Online
http.//www/etecynt.net

ESTA – Entertainment Services and
Technology Association
http://www.esta.org/

IEEE – Institute of Electrical Electronic
Engineers
http://www.ieee.org/

NDCT – National Council for Drama Training
http://www.ncdt.co.uk

PLASA – Professional Lighting and Sound
Association
http://www.plasa.org.uk/

RADA – Royal Academy of Dramatic Art
http://www.rada.org.uk

SBTD – Society of British Theatre Designers
http://www.theatredesign.org.uk

USITT – United States Institute for Theatre
Technology
http://www.ffa.ucalgary.ca/usitt/

Resource Sites

Arts Info Database
http://www.arts-info.co.uk/

Backstage World
http://www.stagelight.se/backstage/

CTI Centre for Textual Studies
http://www.hcu.ox.ac.uk/

Lighting Archive
http://www.psu.edu/dept/theatrearts/archives
/index.html

Lighting Links
http://waapa.cowan.edu.au/lx

The Light Network
http://www.lightnetwork.com

McCoys Guide to Theatre & Performance
Studies
http://www.stetson.edu/departments/csata/
thr_guid.html

The Stage Newspaper
http://www.thestage.co.uk

The Stage Technician's Page
http://www.geocites.com/Broadway/3738/

Strand Archive
http://www.ex.ac.uk/drama/strand/welcom.
html

Techiechick (The Rada technical/production
site)
http://www.techiechick.org/

Technical Theatre Glossary
http://www.ex.ac.uk/drama/tech/glossary/html

The Internet Theatre Bookshop
http://www.stageplays.com

UK Theatre Web
http://www.uktw.co.uk/

The WWW Virtual Library Theatre and Drama
http://www.vl-theatre.com

Manufacturers and Hire Companies

A.C. Lighting Ltd
http://www.aclighting.co.uk

ADB
http://www.adb.be

Avab Scandinavia AB
http://www.avabscand.se

CCT Lighting Ltd
http://www.cctlighting.co.uk

Cereberum Lighting Ltd
http://www.creberum.com

Clay Paky Spa
http://www.claypaky.it

Compulite
http://www.stagetec.co.uk

DHA Lighting Ltd
http://www.dhalighting.co.uk

Flying Pig Systems Ltd
http://www.flyingpig.com

Le Maitre Ltd
http://www.lemaitre.co.uk

Lee Filters
http://www.leefilters.com

Lightfactor Sales
http://www.lightfactor.co.uk

Lighting Technology Group
http://www.lighting-tech.com

Martin Professional PLC
http://www.martin.dk

Modelbox
http://www.modelbox.co.uk

Moving Light Company
http://www.moving-light.co.uk

Northern Light
http://www.northernlight.co.uk

Pani (Ludwig Pani GmbH)
http://www.pani.com

Pulsar Light of Cambridge Ltd
http://www.pulsarlight.com

Rainmaker Ltd
http://www.rainmakerltd.co.uk

Robert Juliat S.A.
http://www.robertjuliat.fr

Romator Rainbow Production AB
http://www.rainbow-colour-changers.de

Rosco
http://www.rosco.com

Selecon
http://www.selecon.co.nz/-selecon

Stage Craft International Inc
http://www.pworld.net.ph/user/stgecrft

Stagecraft Ltd
http://www.stagecraft.co.uk

Stage Electrics
http://www.stage-electrics.co.uk

Strand Lighting
http://www.strandlight.com

Vari-Lite Inc
http://www.vari-lite.com

White Light (Electrics) Ltd
http://www.whitelight.ltd.uk

Zero 88 Lighting Ltd
http://www.zero88.com

INDEX